S0-ABY-476

THE CONTRACEPTION GUIDEBOOK

Other Books by the Authors

Nonfiction

The Infertility Companion

Sexual Intimacy in Marriage

When Empty Arms Become a Heavy Burden:
  Encouragement for Couples Facing Infertility

Fiction

Lethal Harvest

Deadly Cure

False Positive

THE CONTRACEPTION GUIDEBOOK

OPTIONS, RISKS, AND ANSWERS FOR CHRISTIAN COUPLES

WILLIAM R. CUTRER, M.D. & SANDRA L. GLAHN, TH.M.

Christian
Medical
Association
Resources

ZONDERVAN™

GRAND RAPIDS, MICHIGAN 49530 USA

ZONDERVAN™

The Contraception Guidebook
Copyright © 2005 by Sandra L. Glahn and William R. Cutrer

Requests for information should be addressed to:
Zondervan, *Grand Rapids, Michigan 49530*

Library of Congress Cataloging-in-Publication Data

Cutrer, William, 1951–
    The contraception guidebook : options, risks, and answers for christian couples /
William R. Cutrer and Sandra L. Glahn.
       p. cm.
    Includes bibliographical references and index.
    ISBN-10: 0-310-25407-8 (softcover)
    ISBN-13: 978-0-310-25407-2
    1. Contraception—Popular works.   2. Contraception—Religious aspects—Christian-
ity. I. Glahn, Sandra, 1958– . II. Title.
    RG136.2.C88 2005
    613.9'4—dc22

                        2004029111

All Scripture quotations, unless otherwise indicated, are taken from the *Holy Bible: New International Version®*. NIV®. Copyright © 1973, 1978, 1984 by International Bible Society. Used by permission of Zondervan. All rights reserved.

Scripture quotations marked NASB are taken from the NEW AMERICAN STANDARD BIBLE®. Copyright © The Lockman Foundation 1960, 1962, 1963, 1968, 1971, 1973, 1975, 1977, 1995. Used by permission.

Scripture quotations marked KJV are taken from the King James version of the Bible.

The website addresses recommended throughout this book are offered as a resource to you. These websites are not intended in any way to be or imply an endorsement on the part of Zondervan, nor do we vouch for their content for the life of this book.

All rights reserved. No part of this publication may be reproduced, stored in a retrieval system, or transmitted in any form or by any means—electronic, mechanical, photocopy, recording, or any other—except for brief quotations in printed reviews, without the prior permission of the publisher.

Interior design by Michelle Espinoza

Printed in the United States of America

05 06 07 08 09 10 11 /❖ DCI/ 10 9 8 7 6 5 4 3 2 1

To Drs. Steven Harris, Glen Heckman, and Dale Ehmer
colleagues, partners, and brothers in Christ,
physicians for both bodies and souls

CONTENTS

Foreword

Time was nearly everybody agreed that God was in charge of making babies, that families grew out of the union of a male and female who joined hearts as well as bodies in a mystical union. The almighty Creator scheduled birthdays.

Fast-forward to the twenty-first century to a world in which man has said, "Move over, God, we have our own way of doing this. After all, it's only right that we should regulate our own sexuality." And God answers, "I have given you free will, but remember I have already spoken."

"Children," wrote King Solomon in the 127th psalm, "are a heritage from the Lord," a gift, a sign of God's favor. All that is best of human life converges in the delicate innocence of a healthy newborn baby. With our infant's very presence, we connect with generations long past, and for the moment we renew our hopes for good times to come. We marvel at our new addition, our namesake, proof of the power of our love, a joyous herald of bright tomorrows.

With the promise of pedigree, however, Solomon's word *heritage* also carries the connotation of an assignment, a parental responsibility, a stewardship. Solomonic wisdom begins with that cautionary note. "Unless the Lord builds the house, its builders labor in vain"—a hint of downward drag, a yellow warning flag: you cannot do this by yourself. Families face adversity, and although children grace our lives with exquisite joy, the tragedy in the Garden of Eden has exacted its toll. Disobedience disrupted first-family unity, depriving Adam and Eve of their two sons. Only divine intervention in sending a third son, Seth, saved the fragile thread of faith begun by Abel.

Eve would bear children in pain. Adam would earn his living by a lifetime of hard labor. A death sentence hung over the human race. Nothing except God's incalculable act of love in sending his own son, Jesus Christ, as atonement could set the human house in order. The psalmist says he must be the consultant, the active partner in every phase of truly successful marriages and families.

Our current scientific bravado encourages recklessness at the steering wheel of childbirth. Young couples grow up in a world in which matters of love, sex, marriage, and family have been grossly distorted and ill-defined. Obsession with pleasure and do-it-yourself families in the framework of today's tortuous technology pose maternal problems. Critical misunderstanding of factual data have landed many couples in a biological ditch.

Urgently needed is a trustworthy, well-informed guide through the brambles across the door to parenthood. Happily, medical skills and long experience combine to earn Dr. William Cutrer a significant platform from which to instruct all of us on matters of birthing children. I am personally indebted to Dr. Cutrer for his competence in ushering three of my own beautiful healthy grandchildren into this world. In this work, his compassion for young couples struggling with the vagaries of childbirth integrates with a studied adherence to the foundational principles of all human knowledge, the Word of God. His bedside manner in print speaks confidential words of wisdom to deeply personal dilemmas. Drawing upon a broad understanding of emotional and spiritual concerns, his medical treatment lifts parents to draw upon timeless wisdom, confident that God is in control.

The writing team of Cutrer and Glahn has already demonstrated proficiency in translating obstetrical jargon into understandable English in previous books and articles which have been warmly welcomed by many of us who seek to advise others with credible resources. *The Contraception Guidebook* follows in a line of first-rate books on trouble areas of reproduction. Reading them is like sitting in on high-tuition seminars and leaving with the exclamation, "Oh, now I understand!"

Perhaps never before in history has the process of bearing children been surrounded by more perilous ethical and moral challenges. Not only do we need to understand accurately the "what?" of baby-making but the "what for?" What are the basic purposes of our bodies, our circumstances, our gender, and our relationships with those of the opposite gender? Why does God not allow some of us the privilege of procreation? How can we overcome biological barriers? We must become articulate in communicating and modeling our convictions. We dare not say to our younger generation, "Do what you think best and may the Lord bless you." To have or to hold back from having children cannot be a decision made solely on the basis of personal preference and good feelings.

Now that science has placed in human hands the awesome power to regulate family size, the procedure of building a family demands more than human reasoning. Our world at large has always been a dangerous battleground on which to launch our "arrows," as the psalmist puts it, but our times thunder with unprecedented and daunting social, financial, psychological, and spiritual perils never before encountered.

Here is a well-reasoned manual of unmatched proportions. To Sandra Glahn, with whom I am associated at Dallas Theological Seminary, belongs major credit for bringing a distinctive and refreshing perspective to the medical information and theological texts.

Every Christian leader, every marital advisor, indeed everyone who cares about families in our world should include this most important book on the active reading shelf. Cutrer and Glahn come to us for such a time as ours.

—Howard G. Hendricks
Distinguished Professor
Chairman, Center for Christian Leadership
Dallas Theological Seminary

PREFACE

Contraception. Birth control. Family planning. Family building. Say the words and you will almost immediately evoke some strong responses, particularly within the Christian community. Our desire in writing this book is to speak kindness, gentleness, and humility in what has been at times a heated discussion. In attempting to do so, we've outlined some parameters for this work, which we hope readers will find helpful.

Terminology

In this discussion of contraception, we will avoid using the term *birth control* because some people see in that term an ungodly philosophical orientation that suggests humans can control birth, something that ultimately only God can do. Others take offense at the term *family planning*, concerned that it presumes upon the future. For this reason, in this work we use *contraception* when referring to the deliberate prevention of pregnancy and *family building* when discussing conceiving, child spacing, and adoption.[1]

Audience

Our comments will be directed primarily toward married and engaged couples, though we also have in mind pastors, counselors, and teachers. When we speak of building a family, we are talking about a man and women related to each other by marriage and the children who may join them by birth or adoption.

Voice

While this work is a true collaboration, all references in the first person singular should be read as being spoken by Dr. Bill.

Approach

For some people, any discussion or consideration of using contraception is inappropriate. In the minds of these individuals, couples must avoid any technique that might interfere with the potential for conception. Some within this group hold that even abstinence during a woman's midcycle is wrong. They believe that purposefully spacing children or using contraceptives violates God's mandate to "be fruitful and multiply."

At the other end of the spectrum are those who consider all contraceptive methods acceptable. They support the use of even those methods that can destroy a developing embryo.

Somewhere in the middle are those who believe that the Genesis mandate for humans to multiply was a general command that has been fulfilled and is therefore not to be taken as an individual command that still applies to each married believer today. Those in this group condone some, but not all, forms of contraception, insisting that God has given us the technology to influence our own responsible choices and he holds us accountable for managing well the resources he has given us.

We will seek to treat fairly and sensitively the many points of view about contraception, holding each up to the light of Scripture.

Certain questions repeatedly present themselves to anyone who deeply explores this issue:

- Is it "unnatural" to seek to prevent pregnancy? Does it go against God's plan?
- How have the various branches of Christianity dealt with contraception in the past?
- What cultural factors may be blinding us in our biblical interpretation of verses that relate to children being gifts from God?
- Must sexual intimacy always be accompanied by the potential to reproduce?
- Does "spiritual reproduction" (making disciples) take precedence over physical reproduction?

In exploring these questions, we will assume some presuppositions:

- All human life, even at the one-cell stage, is created in God's image and is deserving of respect and the full rights of personhood. All decisions regarding contraception must uphold the sanctity of human life (Ex. 20:13). Scripture is clear in saying that each individual is unique, created in God's image, and of inestimable worth.
- The Bible is our ultimate authority (2 Tim. 3:16). When it comes to specific instructions about contraception, we can't cite some verse in Leviticus or 1 John that gives a definitive biblical answer about what to do. Yet there *is* a way to reason issues from the Scriptures, even when we find no direct statements about those issues. In such cases, rather than finding absolutes, we see general scriptural principles. And where principles are concerned, there will be some variance in practice (Rom. 14:1–12; 1 Cor. 8:4–13). In this work, we will reason from Scripture as often and as carefully as we can, but where the Bible is silent, we'll acknowledge that silence.
- Believers are promised guidance through the Holy Spirit (Rom. 5:5; James 1:5).

To these presuppositions, we would add another:

- A child is a precious gift from God. A child, however, is not the *ultimate* gift from God. Not every couple is called to, or is able to, procreate. Only God's ultimate gift, Jesus Christ—and life in him—is offered to all. We agree with the position that "God has allowed some couples to be without biological children according to His sovereign plan in their lives. We believe couples without children are of no less value before God than those with children."[2]

Experience suggests that God has given large families to some, small families to others, and has called yet others to remain single. In fact, living a single, celibate life for the sake of gospel ministry appears to be a special calling (1 Cor. 7:7). Clearly, having children does not define our purpose as human beings. Many faithful saints of God—including the Lord himself—remained both celibate and childless.

This work is not a defense for large families; nor is it our intention to argue in defense of contraception. Scripture reveals that God has promised to give his children wisdom from above if we will ask for it (James 1:5). And Jesus promised to send the Comforter, the Holy Spirit, as our guide, so we are not left to our own imaginations. We encourage readers to draw on these resources—the Spirit and his guidance—as we explore together the issues associated with God's blueprint for building a godly house. We do not presume that the specific plan and wisdom God reveals to an individual or couple is to be considered universally applicable to others.

Unless the LORD builds the house, its builders labor in vain.
—Psalm 127:1

Note: Many people have shared their experiences and thoughts with us, and we have included quotations from these people throughout the book, set in italics. At times we have edited their wording to protect identities or to fit in the allotted space.

ACKNOWLEDGMENTS

In Nehemiah 3, we read a long list of names that includes everyone—down to the perfume workers—who helped to rebuild the wall of Jerusalem. Often a great effort requires a few people who are seen front and center and a large group of people willing to serve behind the scenes. *The Contraception Guidebook* is no exception. And while we would like to publicly thank all who have influenced this work, many must remain unnamed due to the sensitive nature of the material. We are, nevertheless, grateful to them. We acknowledge the contributions of the many men and women who have entrusted to us their experiences—whether we've met in doctors' offices, in hospitals, at radio stations, in churches, at conferences, through our website, or whether they are friends or family members. Their desire to honor God even in the most private areas of their lives has been an inspiration and a motivation for this work.

In terms of book production, we are deeply indebted to our friend, Gene Rudd, M.D., of the Christian Medical Association, without whose friendship, counsel, encouragement, advocacy, suggestions, and comments this book would have been impossible. We are also grateful to Cindy Lambert Hays at Zondervan, whose expertise, vision, and commitment to this project have significantly influenced it for the better.

Thanks are also due to Kathy Anderegg, M.D., for her willing and competent assistance with the research; to our webmaster, Mike Justice, Th.M., who has done much to expand the borders of our ministry; to Keith Yates, M.A. (B.S.), for providing the medical drawings; and to our readers and editors, Jane Cutrer, Gregg Albers, M.D., Will Gunnels, M.Div., Brian Phipps, Robert Scheidt, M.D., Barbara Snapp, and Lynn Wilson.

Finally, we are grateful most of all for our spouses, Jane Cutrer and Gary Glahn, for their loyal love, their constant encouragement, and their continuing partnership in this and all of our ministries.

PART I

MYTHS AND FACTS

CHAPTER 1

HOW MANY CHILDREN DO YOU WANT?

How many children do you want?

For more than twenty years, when engaged couples have come to me for premarital counsel—either in my capacity as a physician or as a pastor—I have asked them to sit back to back so they can't see each other's response and then have asked them to raise the number of fingers for the number of children they hope to have. Rarely have both the man and woman given the same answer.

This exercise helps many couples realize that in their plans for marriage, an important consideration has been left out. "How many?" and "When?" can be complex questions.

- An engaged woman attending a Christian college overhears one of her professors explaining why he has six children: "We don't use contraception—that would mean a lack of faith. We prefer to trust God." She wonders how she and her fiancé will balance "stepping out in faith" with weighing the pros and cons and making wise decisions.
- A wife has been using the pill, but she and her husband recently heard that the pill causes abortion by killing the early embryo. Now they have second thoughts and are trying to figure out what method of contraception, if any, is best for them.
- Feeling her biological clock ticking, a wife is eager to stop using contraception. Her husband, concerned to first establish

financial security, wants to wait. Their endless discussions about when to stop using contraception are getting them nowhere.

- A couple with five children have always thought it was wrong to use contraception but have now been told that the wife's health would be endangered if she were to have another child. They have no idea where to begin in considering the options.
- An engaged couple plans to use contraception after they marry, but they have no idea what options are available and which ones fit within their pro-life beliefs.

Each of the individuals in these situations has desired to honor God with his or her choices, so they have turned to Scripture for guidance. There they've found much written about living sexually pure lives but nothing directly about contraception—the deliberate prevention of pregnancy.

Some people assume that the Bible is silent about contraception because it did not exist in Bible times. Yet some methods, such as withdrawal, have been around for thousands of years, as we will discuss. This raises even more questions. Is the Bible silent on the subject because it is a relatively unimportant issue? Or were certain practices assumed?

In exploring such questions, we will draw on our theological training and our discussions with hundreds of couples. In addition, my many years of medical practice as an obstetrician and gynecologist, my experience in pastoral ministry, and my years of teaching at the seminary level provide case studies and quotes that come from real-life encounters.

LET'S TALK ABOUT IT

1. How many children do you want? How many children does your spouse want?
2. Is there a difference between the two numbers?
3. Did you know this before you married?
4. Have either of your changed your minds about this since you married?

5. Have you come to a consensus about family building? If not, what needs to happen for you to find a place of oneness?

6. In general, how do you as a couple handle conflict resolution? Would you say you "find one another's heart"? Does one of you tend to give in while the other gets his or her way? Do you both seek unity and godliness through love? If not, what steps need to be taken to move in that direction?

CHAPTER 2

YOU WON'T
GET PREGNANT IF . . .

Sometime in early childhood, we get wise. We find out about the Tooth Fairy, the Easter Bunny, and Santa Claus. Such knowledge then casts serious doubt on the Birds and the Bees, the Cabbage Patch, and the Stork. Ultimately, the moment our parents have anticipated (and some have dreaded) arrives: "Mommy? Daddy? Where did I come from?"

At this point, wise parents pause to ask a few questions before forging into details in case—as the joke goes—their youngster merely wants to know if he is from California, like the new neighbors. Unfortunately, the reverse is the more common scenario: Mom and Dad are too late. Before they have a chance to pass along the facts about sex in any consistent, systematic way, the neighborhood kids have already revealed the Big Secret. When it comes to questions about sexuality and sexual behavior, most young people seek out siblings, cousins, the internet, even television cartoons, as their primary sources for the Answer.

Eventually, folklore about sex, learned on the playground or later in the locker room, passes for fact in the back seat of a car and in the bedroom. And the related topic of contraception is certainly no exception. Ignorance and misrepresentation have long histories here. A few highlights from the past will let us know that entire generations have outdone us in being uninformed and gullible.

The Things We Do for Love

Early historical records reveal some repugnant methods of contraception. In fact, just reading about them can evoke nausea. There's no question that when actually used, many of these methods would have killed sexual desire. Consider, for example, that about two thousand years ago Egyptian women dipped crocodile-dung tampons in honey, onion juice, and mint sap. This unique concoction was stuffed into the vagina to block the passage of sperm. Beyond crocodile-dung inserts, progress in contraception included vaginal suppositories made of cocoa butter and various chemicals to plug up the cervix and kill any sperm that came near. Swallowing live tadpoles was a Chinese approach to contraception, while others favored eating the scrapings from inside a deer's antlers. Innumerable creative yet biologically unsound (and often medically unsafe) contraceptive techniques existed. Clearly, a mutual commitment was involved before agreeing to slurp down a tadpole or to insert animal matter into one's body.

The Greeks and Romans reportedly soaked cloth tampons in hemlock and quinine, figuring the sperm couldn't survive such an insult. The women's vaginal tissues would easily allow absorption of some of the poison as well. Saxon women used roasted horse manure to generate an aroma that would be detrimental to the sperm. (No doubt it also extinguished the paramour's burning fire, another effective means of contraception.) When the aroma of eau de Seabiscuit wafted through the bedroom, a woman's lover knew it was "time."

Also on the list of international barrier techniques were balls of bamboo tissue paper, the Japanese prostitutes' method of choice. Islamic and Greek women used balls of wool, while Slavic women used linen rags.[1] The idea was to soak up the little swimmers, but they are tenacious, persistent, and clearly goal oriented.

In Italy, male contraception included a moistened linen sheath wrapped around the erect penis and tied with a pink ribbon. But, alas, linen works poorly as a barrier to sperm. So while the ribbon wrap may have had aesthetic advantages over latex condoms, it undoubtedly was ineffective. Early condoms in the seventeenth century were made from animal intestines tied off at one end, an approach that can be effective and that persists in parts of the world today. Both the rubber condom and the diaphragm came on the scene in the second half of the nineteenth century. These early barrier methods were the precursors of today's barrier methods, which have improved steadily in texture and reliability.

To the best of our knowledge, the earliest intrauterine devices were created in an ancient animal lab. Nomads traveling the deserts noticed that inserting a foreign object (some claim it was a peach pit) into a camel's uterus would prevent one's mode of transportation from conceiving. We wonder what brave and brilliant nomad was the first to contemplate and then try this theory. And what objects were unsuccessful? Did some camels have to endure mangoes, watermelon pits, small stones, or coins?

Early forms of our modern intrauterine devices (IUDs) were used in humans beginning around 1900. About twenty years later, "birth control clinics" began to open under a wave of controversy. They were available only to married women—or soon-to-be-married women—with documentation required. In the 1960s, a university health clinic opened in Scotland under a storm of moral outrage. As one professor protested, the university was "for education, *not* fornication."

Sometimes when it's too late to avoid pregnancy, people have practiced, and still practice, infanticide (the killing of infants). This is done to favor boys who work the land, to reduce the number of children in areas with limited food supplies, and to avoid paying a dowry to daughters' intended spouses. Various potions have been concocted to induce abortion. These include herbs (such as marjoram, thyme, parsley, and lavender) as well as recipes from animal sources such as mashed ants, camel spit, and hair of the black-tailed deer. More recently, women have tried to abort pregnancies by swallowing such substances as turpentine, castor oil, quinine water, Epsom salts, and ammonia.[2]

While young women in the past were told that marjoram, thyme, and parsley could kill a child, today's young women hear that pregnancy will not result from engaging in certain sexual activities. We have compiled a list of some of these myths.

Truth or Consequences?

Much of what follows has originated from those trying to have sex outside of marriage. Yet many of these myths are now so widely circulated that we felt it important to set the record straight (comments from individuals and couples appear hereafter in nonbold italics).

Myth: You can't get pregnant the first time you have sex.

Fact: Yes, you can get pregnant the first time you have sex.

The first time I had sex, I got pregnant.

I started my period right before I turned twelve. I never had very regular periods and was put on birth control pills for this. The doctor put me on a low-dose pill, and I didn't know it wasn't as effective as a stronger one, so I ended up pregnant the first time I had sex. I had a baby two months after I turned fifteen.

Sperm reaching the egg is what causes pregnancy, so it doesn't matter if it's the first time you've had sex or the thousandth. The only absolute way to avoid pregnancy is to abstain from sexual relations.

Myth: You can't get pregnant if you have sex standing up, or if the woman is on top, or if you're underwater, or if the woman doesn't experience orgasm.

Fact: The opposite of each of these statements is true. You can get pregnant if you have sex standing up, if the woman is on top, if you're underwater, and if the woman doesn't experience orgasm. Gravity and water are minor inconveniences to target-driven sperm. Once sperm reach the cervical mucus (within seconds of male orgasm), a woman can turn cartwheels without confusing the sperm, as they are on a mission. The underwater theory presumes that water will wash out the sperm, or that salty, soapy, or chlorinated water will kill the sperm. Yet once the sperm hit the cervical mucus (which is within *seconds* of ejaculation within the vagina), they are relatively safe. They won't drown, nor do they need to tread water. They have tails and are described in medicine as "swimming." Counting on chlorinated water, salt water, or bathwater to interfere with the steady progress toward the egg is foolhardy.

As for a connection between female orgasm and pregnancy, millions of women have conceived without experiencing orgasm. Some believe that when a woman achieves climax after the man does, fertility may be slightly increased due to enhanced sperm movement caused by a small suction effect that pulls the sperm into the woman's uterus. There's a certain logic behind this theory. Yet while studies have shown that such a tiny vacuum effect exists, whether that translates to higher pregnancy rates remains unproven.

Myth: A woman can't get pregnant if she's having her period.

Fact: Many women have conceived during menstruation. A woman's fertile time is at ovulation. Some women have shorter-than-average cycles, which means the egg is released (or ovulated) earlier than in other women's cycles. That is, a woman who cycles every twenty-eight days (assuming the first day of menstruation is day one) will be fertile around day fourteen. But if she cycles regularly at twenty-two days, she will be fertile around day eight.

Let's say a woman with a twenty-two-day cycle flows and spots for five or six days and has intercourse near the end of this time frame. Keep in mind that sperm live at least three days and up to five days. (Some experts even estimate that sperm live for a week!) Thus, intercourse on day seven may well result in live sperm in the area of the ovaries all the way up to day fourteen.

In addition, many women occasionally spot at midcycle. If a woman wrongly assumes such spotting indicates that she has started her period and she has sex, she will have actually engaged in relations during her most fertile time.

Due to the extreme variability of the length of women's cycles and even month-to-month variability in individual women's cycles, the potential for pregnancy can be present at any time.

Myth: A woman can't get pregnant if the penis is never inserted into the vagina.

Fact: Sperm will find a way. If the ejaculate touches the moist areas around the vagina, the sperm can find their way through the vagina to the cervix, and the journey begins. So-called outercourse, in which penetration doesn't occur but ejaculation bathes the vulva, is very risky. More than one of my patients has conceived without vaginal penetration. Couples who manually stimulate each other to climax often get ejaculate on their hands, garments, and bedsheets. Subsequent vaginal contact can bring sperm in touch with the woman's cervical mucus. Leakage of ejaculate following anal intercourse can also result in pregnancy.

Myth: Withdrawing the penis just before ejaculation will prevent pregnancy.

Fact: While withdrawal, known as *coitus interruptus*, is probably the most time-tested (and affordable) method of family spacing, it has little to commend it. First, most men have a pre-ejaculate—a clear bit of fluid that precedes the full ejaculation. The pre-ejaculate is rich in sperm. Thus, even if a man pulls out in the nick of time, it may be too late because the pre-ejaculate sperm are already deposited in the vagina. In addition, counting on a man to withdraw his penis just before ejaculation requires trusting him to exert a remarkable amount of control—at a moment in which every fiber of his being is screaming to stay and savor the pleasurable sensations that God designed to accompany orgasm during penetration. This method is frustrating for both husband and wife.

I have treated many couples in my medical practice who used this technique for years without conceiving, but I do not recommend it. I have also treated many couples who practiced this method and soon afterward required my obstetrical skills.

Myth: Everyone knows how to use a condom.

Fact: More than half of all pregnancies in America are unintended—and more than half of those happen when contraception is being used.[3] And where condoms are concerned, more pregnancies result from improper use than from condom breakage.

Because of the pre-ejaculate, the condom must be put on the erect penis before vaginal contact. Condoms are manufactured with a reservoir at the tip so that the sperm can be collected and the force of the ejaculation won't rupture the condom. After ejaculation, the penis must be removed from the vagina. The man must hold the condom in place on his still-erect penis so that it doesn't slip or leak. Many couples, basking in the glow of the endorphin surge, forget this critical step. As a result, when the penis becomes flaccid, the semen leaks directly into the vagina. The condom has done its job, but its user's failure has reduced the level of protection.

In addition, condoms deteriorate rapidly with exposure to air, humidity, light, and heat. Thus, a condom stored in a glove compartment or one with torn packaging is prone to break and leak. Moreover, many condom users forget that contact with petroleum-based lubricants, such as mineral oil, Vaseline, massage oils, and baby oil, may damage latex within three to four minutes, which increases the risk of breakage.

Myth: Douching, bathing, or showering after sex will prevent pregnancy.

Fact: Done for centuries, douching (washing out the vagina) after sex is an ineffective means of contraception, though some interesting combinations of liquids have been tried. Once sperm have already come in contact with cervical mucus (seconds after intercourse), it is impossible to wash them out or to kill them. By the time intercourse is over and a woman begins to douche or bathe, the sperm are secure within the protective mucus. People have douched with all sorts of substances, including bleach, Lysol, and Coca-Cola. The theory that these chemicals will wash out sperm and work as a spermicide underestimates the safety of the cervical mucus. Medically speaking, spraying these materials inside the vagina carries significant risk of infection and may result in fertility problems in the future, while still failing to prevent pregnancy.

Myth: A girl can't get pregnant until she starts menstruating.

Fact: This seems logical because ovulation precedes menstruation, but every woman has to release that first egg, and that first ovulation will precede her first period. Many young girls have spotting and irregular bleeding before they begin ovulatory cycles, but one shouldn't assume she is not ovulating. Thus, a woman can conceive during her first ovulation, before her first genuine period.

Myth: You can't conceive while you're nursing.

Fact: While nursing may have a contraceptive effect for some women, for others it doesn't. It's true that most women who are nursing around the clock will not ovulate, so there is some validity to this approach. Some cultures that have no available contraceptive methods rely totally on lactation amenorrhea (an absence of periods while the mother is nursing), but unless the mother wants to nurse the child around the clock until he's a preschooler (and some do), nursing is not a reliable means of contraception.

The road from dung to diaphragms has been long and bumpy—and not necessarily always one of progress. Some have exchanged linen for Lysol, and tadpoles for soft drinks—none of which works. Still, a variety of safe and effective contraceptive products are available today. And a simple education about how a woman's body signals her fertile time is necessary for understanding how contraception works.

LET'S TALK ABOUT IT

1. Which, if any, of the above myths and facts had you already heard?
2. Which did you find most amusing?
3. Which did you find most unappealing?
4. Which did you find to be the most plausible?
5. From whom did you learn the facts of life? Would you say you received an accurate education?

CHAPTER 3

THE WHY OF SEX

What They Didn't Teach Us in Health Class

May your fountain be blessed,
*   and may you rejoice in the wife of your youth.*
A loving doe, a graceful deer—
*   may her breasts satisfy you always,*
*   may you ever be captivated by her love.*
*   —Proverbs 5:18–19*

Strengthen me with raisins,
*   refresh me with apples,*
*   for I am faint with love.*
His left arm is under my head,
*   and his right arm embraces me.*
*   —Song of Songs 2:5–6*

You are a garden fountain,
*   a well of flowing water*
*   streaming down from Lebanon.*
Awake, north wind,
*   and come south wind!*
Blow on my garden,
*   that its fragrance may spread abroad.*
Let my lover come into his garden
*   and taste its choice fruits.*
*   —Song of Songs 4:15–16*

If this stuff weren't in the Bible, most parents wouldn't let their kids read it. The expressions of romance and intimacy found throughout the Old Testament encourage people of faith that God created sexual pleasure for full expression and enjoyment within marriage. God created male and female, brought the man and woman together, and then declared all of creation "very good" (Gen. 1:31). Clearly, making sex distinctions was part of the divine design.

In Genesis 2, we read that a man leaves his mother and father and cleaves to his wife, and the two become "one flesh" (2:24). This one-flesh picture includes sexual union, but it encompasses much more than that. It suggests a level of intimacy and interconnectedness in all of life. In the next verse, we read that the man and his wife were both "naked and unashamed" (2:25, our trans.).

In the Beginning . . .

Before sin entered the picture, man and woman experienced a perfect environment, perfect fellowship with their Creator, and genuine intimacy with one another. Their nakedness—physical and emotional—caused no shame, only oneness. This remains the ideal.

When sin entered the world, however, pride, self-centeredness, blame, and shame came with it. Sexual intimacy and marital oneness suffered. Part of the result, directed at the woman but also affecting the man, was the decree that she would have pain associated with childbearing. What could have been natural, smooth, and relatively painless became "labor."

Then the biblical text records that God predicts the woman will "desire" her husband and he will "rule" over her (3:16). Both this context and later use of the word "desire" suggest it means an unhealthy desire to dominate (4:7). And the idea of "rule" conjures up images of power that plays out within the marriage context.[1] What God designed as a unifying, satisfying experience—sexuality and sexual intimacy in marriage—became a major source of pain and conflict.

Along with the responsibility for exercising dominion over the earth, God gave the first couple the responsibility and privilege of filling the earth. Sexual intercourse was part of that divinely ordained process. Even today, most of us learn relatively early that it takes a man and a woman to reproduce.[2]

The Purpose of Sex: Two Schools

Why did God create sex? What did he intend as its purposes? It has many purposes, but is there a main one? Two main schools of thought exist, and they differ in their views of the reasons or purposes for marriage:

1. The purpose (or primary purpose) of marriage is to unite two people for reproduction, or "procreation." Both the "unitive" aspect (the uniting, or the act of intercourse) and the procreative (reproductive) aspect of marital love must always be present and never be separated in each sex act. This is called the "unitive-procreative link."
2. The purpose (or primary purpose) of marriage is to reflect the intimacy between Christ and his bride, the church. Intimate knowledge is at the core of that image. Procreation is often, but not always, a part of that picture.

Some proponents of the first group, those who believe the unitive-procreative link must always be present, believe any form of contraception is inappropriate. For them, even scheduled abstinence is seen as potentially interfering with God's blessing. Yet most people that hold to this view consider natural family planning (NFP) a viable option. We have included information about how to access the Vatican statement (see the resources section at the back of the book) as representative of this view, and we encourage readers to read it thoughtfully.

Many others hold to the second point of view, which sees Scripture as teaching something different—that the primary purpose of sex is intimate knowledge. We will review a variety of perspectives without advocating any of them.

Both the unitive-procreative model and the "knowing" model appreciate the gift of sexual expression within marriage as the joyful pathway to husband-wife intimacy. But in the second model, while procreation may be a part of this picture, it is not the key to this picture. It's not the main purpose of sex. Thus, contraception may be appropriate, because intimate knowledge can be deepened even when conception is unlikely or even impossible. This school of thought fully supports sexual expression within marriage for the pregnant, sterile, elderly, and postmenopausal. According to this view, God designed marital sexual expression to be enjoyed throughout the seasons of life because it deepens knowledge—of one's spouse, of one's self, and of the relationship. And it even expresses something about God and our ability to know and love him and to be fully known and fully loved by him.

Those who hold to a unitive-procreative model believe that at least the potential for procreation must be present in each sexual encounter. This mindset influences many teachings relating to contraceptives, manual sex, oral sex, and reproductive technologies. This is the official position of the Roman Catholic Church, though others hold to it as well.

Both systems stem from scholars' desires to assess faithfully God's intention for the marriage bed—considerations sorely lacking in our culture at large. How many couples stop and ask themselves, "How can we best honor God in our intimate life?"

Any couple thinking about getting married would be wise to explore this topic thoroughly before saying their vows. Do they themselves and those responsible for their spiritual well-being see marriage as having an inseparable unitive-procreative link (and thus contraception as unethical)? Or do they believe the purpose of sex is "knowing," with some flexibility where contraception is concerned?

The Purpose of Sex as "Knowing"

In his weekly weblog, Dr. Al Mohler, president of the Southern Baptist Seminary, summarized the problem many people have with the belief that procreation—or at least the potential for procreation—must be present in every sex act: "[For most Protestants,] the major break with Catholic teaching comes at the insistence that 'it is necessary that each conjugal act remain ordained in itself to the procreating of human life.' That is, that every act of marital intercourse must be fully and equally open to the gift of children." Dr. Mohler feels this claims too much and places too much emphasis on individual acts of sexual intercourse. "The focus on 'each and every act' of sexual intercourse within a faithful marriage that is open to the gift of children goes beyond the biblical demand," he says. Because the Roman Catholic Church does not reject all family planning, Mohler feels they are forced to therefore make an odd "distinction between 'natural' and 'artificial' methods of birth control. To the evangelical mind, this is a rather strange and fabricated distinction."[3]

Scriptural Observations

Several chapters into Genesis, we read about the first sexual encounter: "And Adam knew Eve his wife; and she conceived" (Gen. 4:1 KJV). Modern translations say that Adam "lay with" or "had relations with" his wife, but the older translations were closer to the original: "knew." Sexual intimacy at its foundation is about knowing.

Thumbing ahead to Song of Songs, we find the only book of the Bible that's devoted to marital sexual love. Interestingly enough, we find no mention of children in the entire book. So it appears that in addition to populating the planet, God intended sex to have other purposes as well. Later, in the New Testament, the apostle Paul exhorts husbands and wives to give themselves fully to each other lest they be tempted by sustained abstinence (1 Cor. 7:5). Again we find no mention of procreation. Instead, we see a husband's and a wife's responsibility to meet each other's ongoing sexual needs.

The fact that we find marital sexual intimacy presented this way—without reference to procreation—suggests that the purpose of sex, while including procreation, also involves unity and pleasure. It meets a need. In fact, for most couples, procreative seasons represent a relatively small portion of their entire married lives.

Observations from God's Created World

Many in the annals of church history believed sex was designed solely (or primarily) for procreation. But Aristotle, who believed women to be inferior to men, influenced much of early Christian thought in the Roman world. Today much of that thinking has been challenged in light of what Scripture teaches about God creating both man and woman in his image. In addition, we have access to information from the realms of biology and physiology that was unavailable to theologians of the past. Had they known what we know now, they might have thought differently on the subject.

For example, Aquinas thought life began at quickening (when the mother first feels fetal motion). He lacked the benefit we have of ultrasound equipment and the findings of embryology, which might have altered his view. Centuries later, Puritans passed laws forbidding women to enjoy sex. If the women so much as smiled during the act, she might find herself sent to stand in the wooden stocks. Many theologians of the past held that even marital sex was potentially sinful but a necessary evil to accomplish procreation. Most scholars today believe God intended for pleasure to be a significant part of the sexual act.

More Myths

During childhood, we pick up information and attitudes about our bodies. By the time we reach adolescence, we are bombarded with messages about our bodies and especially about sex. And much of the information is untrue. Consider the following myths that many people believed in past centuries:

- Men can't control themselves. It's up to the girl to keep things cool.
- Good girls are never in the mood.
- God's ideal for sex is that it should happen only in the missionary position, lights out, under the covers, clothed in flannel, on Saturday night. A couple should try not to enjoy the fleshly union too much, lest they sin. Instead, they should see it as their duty to God to procreate.
- Women by nature have a much stronger desire for sex than men do, and women use their wiles to hide their sexual desire. But beware!

Or what about these more recently held myths:

- As long as the man uses a condom, you can't get sexually transmitted infections.
- Oral sex isn't really sex.
- It's okay to have sex when you're not married as long as you love each other.

Today's youth learn some information about sex from siblings and parents, who provide spoken and unspoken information. The television set pipes information about sexual intimacy into the living room. And as young people develop, peers and dating relationships provide even more data. Secular health classes provide information on the mechanics of sex, but they leave out the divinely ordained context for sex: marriage. After a couple announces their engagement, they have reason to learn even more about sex and how their bodies work. At this point, they may endure hearing all sorts of unsolicited advice, much of which is unhelpful and inaccurate. All this information—myths mixed with facts—they bring into the marriage.

God's Design for Sexual Intimacy

Beyond sexual health and satisfaction, a couple must make decisions about their future families. They should consider how many children they want. And they should consider which, if any, methods of contraception to use. They will base their decisions, to some degree, on their understanding of how their bodies work.

The study of modern reproductive physiology, that wonderful science that explores God's design for human reproductive function, demonstrates that God designed sex to be pleasurable, not only for men but for women as well. Consider the following:

- Unlike the penis, the woman's clitoris—her nerve center for experiencing sexual pleasure—serves no function in human reproduction.
- The location of the clitoris is such that most women do not experience ultimate satisfaction from vaginal penetration alone but through other or additional forms of sexual pleasuring. Even after altering positions and controlling the tempo of lovemaking, most women find that to experience orgasm, they need more direct clitoral stimulation than penetration provides. In a study of Christian women, 59 percent said they were unable to experience orgasm during intercourse. (The percentage for Christian women who experience orgasm during intercourse is higher than that of women in the population at large). Most of the women in the study said they reach ultimate satisfaction by their own hand, by their partner's hand, or by oral stimulation. Others use vibrators. A smaller percentage of women rely on external penile stimulation. The very existence of the clitoris and female sexual

response argues for a purpose in sexual intimacy apart from having children. A woman doesn't need to experience an orgasm to conceive, and she can achieve orgasm even when not at all fertile.

- A woman's capacity for experiencing multiple orgasms serves no apparent reproductive function.
- Some who believe in evolution have argued that the reason men reach orgasm quickly is because of the so-called survival advantage in procreating. Men on average can go from excitation to orgasm within several minutes, while women on average require twenty minutes or longer. The rationale has been that in the evolutionary process, men had to reach orgasm quickly because they were vulnerable to outside predators during the sex act. Why, then, have women persisted in a slower mode? Why do women have a sexual response at all? Why can women get pregnant without orgasm? Women's slower, more relational approach suggests a Designer who intended sex to have an added dimension beyond mere procreation: intimacy.

The Number One Sexual Problem

Today the number one sexual problem is talking about it. Often even grown-ups have difficulty talking about their bodies without feeling odd, embarrassed, or even ashamed—despite a culture of openness that includes shock radio and numerous ads for Viagra, Levitra, and Cialis. As Gavin de Becker, the author of *Protecting the Gift*, wrote, "You could fill a book with the sounds and phrases families have coined to avoid saying these three words: vagina, penis, and rectum. The vernacular consists of cute terms like boom-boom, popo, hoosie-doose (yes, that's a real one), poo-poo, wee-wee, and the ever-versatile pee-pee. Even the least creative people seem to flourish when it comes to finding ways to prevent their young son or daughter from saying vagina."[4]

> *If you look in the dictionary, it says "weenie" means "hot dog" and "booty" means "plunder." Somebody needs to let the editors know those aren't the primary meanings of those words in many homes.*

If you want to better communicate your love to your husband or wife, begin by using accurate names for the most intimate parts of your own body, and then learn about your spouse's body too. Discover how God made each of you. What causes a woman's monthly cycle? What do testosterone and estrogen do? You can begin by reading the chapters that follow.

Sex is God's good gift to humans, and he intended sex only for married people. One reason for making it exclusive is because it is so intimate. Two bodies are joined together as one through the act of sex, which is the "dessert" that follows the main entrée of emotional and spiritual oneness. That entrée is served as husbands and wives serve one another, sharing life together.

Happily married couples make sex a priority. As the decades unfold, relational intimacy, as part of the act of physical pleasure, should grow deeper. The wise husband and wife approach the sexual relationship as lifelong learners, noticing and responding to changes in each other's responsiveness as their bodies and circumstances change through the years. Young couples dream of growing old together. Doing that well requires improving communication skills over time and learning how to skillfully touch each other. How does he like to be rubbed? How does she want to be caressed? With appropriate guidance from each other, husbands and wives learn to give and receive pleasure as they keep the embers of their romantic fire glowing. Their skill, along with kindness, tenderheartedness, and forgiveness (Eph. 4:32) provides the backdrop for meaningful, exciting sexual experiences that encompass a couple's entire being for a lifetime.

LET'S TALK ABOUT IT

1. Do you lean more toward viewing the primary purpose of sex as being procreation or knowing? Why?
2. Do you feel comfortable calling body parts by their actual names? Why or why not? Would your spouse give the same answer?
3. How can you improve your marital communication, especially as it relates to sex?

CHAPTER 4

How Our Bodies Work

A re you ready for a quick test? *What is the single most important sexual organ?* As you consider the best answer to that question, consider how amazingly complex the human body is and the vast differences between the male and female bodies. A few more questions to consider: *How does conception actually happen? At what point does life actually begin? Where does that occur? Do contraception methods prevent conception, or do some prevent an already conceived embryo from implanting?* As you can see, before we leap into a discussion of contraception methods, risks, and choices, we would be wise to review how our sexual organs and the conception of new life actually work.

The Brain: the Vital Sex Organ
Brain Sex

Research in neuroanatomy and neurochemistry helps us understand what lovers have known since the beginning: sex can be a powerful, overwhelmingly wonderful experience! The brain releases both chemicals that increase sexual drive and response[1] and ones that decrease libido and performance.[2] Following human climax, the brain releases in large quantities a chemical (endorphins) with the euphoric and sedating qualities of a narcotic. No wonder many people get lost in the quest for the ultimate erotic physical experience and miss the powerful relational impact of sexual intimacy.

Neurology

Male and female sexual responses differ in several ways. As mentioned earlier, the average time from excitation to climax is much shorter for men than for women. And at the level of neuro-logical response, the male climax generally produces an enormous spike of endorphins—perhaps a 200 percent increase—while the female response may range between a similar huge surge and more of a gentle wave that generates a mellow glow.[3]

The obvious physical anatomical differences between men and women indicate the marvelous design of our Creator. The penis and vagina are perfectly fitted (in most couples) to deliver the sperm to the vicinity of the cervical mucus, where hardy sperm can begin the long journey in the quest for the egg. A man's ability to achieve a functional erection and appropriate ejaculation is crucial to fertility.[4]

In the male body, nerve fibers are concentrated in primarily one place for intense sensual pleasure—the head (glans) of the penis. For most men, then, peak sensual pleasure involves vaginal pene-tration, which stimulates vast numbers of these nerves. The woman's corresponding collection of nerves resides in the clitoris, located above the vagina.

As noted earlier, a woman can conceive without ever experi-encing orgasm. For that matter, some women have conceived with-out vaginal penetration. Sperm deposited in or near the vulva have an uncanny ability to find their way into the vagina, through the cervix, uterus, and tubes to seek out the egg. Generally speaking, though, conception occurs through vaginal intercourse and ejaculation.

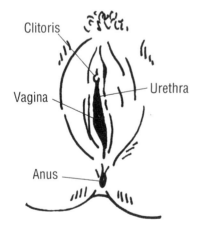

Most contraceptive techniques, then, work to block the progress of sperm or to prevent egg release. Some methods interfere with the reproductive process after concep-tion but before implantation. (We will discuss all of this in detail later.) Researchers are working on some newer methods that change the process of sperm production.

Hormones: His and Hers

Besides the brain chemistry and neurological effects involved in reproduction, the body secretes hormones from various glands throughout the body. These hormones and their effects on fertility and libido constitute a major piece of the conception-contraception puzzle.

Hers

The dominant female hormone, estrogen, is secreted mostly by the ovaries, though estrogen-like compounds can be produced in other tissues, such as fat. Estrogen is responsible for a woman's feminization, such as fatty breast and hip deposits, and for a gentle increase in the libido. A woman's estrogen level rises as the ovary prepares to ovulate, or release the egg, an essential component to pregnancy and a key target for contraceptive approaches. The rising estrogen level has effects throughout a woman's body, which can give clues to fertility. Blocking its rise can prevent ovulation.

A secondary female hormone is progesterone (*pro* = favoring; *gest* = gestation or pregnancy). This hormone increases soon after the egg is released (see chart on p. 60) and causes bodily changes in the woman, some of which she can observe. It is responsible for the bloating, feeling of fullness, and general crankiness that some women experience near the end of their menstrual cycles. Yet to understand reproduction, it's important to know that progesterone also prepares the uterus so that the developing embryo has a lush landing zone where it can implant and thrive. Altering the levels of this hormone is central to some contraceptive (and even abortifacient—that is, abortion inducing) approaches to family planning.

His

For the man, the key hormone is testosterone. As one man put it, "If there is such a thing as a bodily substance more fabled than blood, it's testosterone, the hormone that we understand and misunderstand as the essence of manhood. Testosterone has been offered as the symbolic (and sometimes literal) explanation for all the glories and infamies of men, for why they start street fights and civil wars, for why they channel surf, explore, prevail, sleep around, drive too fast, plunder, bellow, joust, plot corporate takeovers and paint their bare torsos blue during the Final Four. Hey, what's not to like? . . . Who can say no to something that sounds like an Italian dessert named after a Greek god?"[5]

Men also produce estrogen, but women's levels are approximately ten times higher than men's. Likewise, women produce testosterone, but in limited quantities.

The testicles make testosterone in response to a messenger hormone sent from the pituitary gland: LH (luteinizing hormone). Hormone levels can directly affect a man's sperm count and libido. Any contraceptive approach that drastically lowers testosterone or blocks LH, however, has unsatisfactory side effects. In addition, the time from the beginning of sperm production in the testicles to actual ejaculation can take up to three months. Thus, whatever we do to sperm production today won't alter fertility for months. This is an important reason why male hormonal contraceptive approaches have been relatively unsuccessful so far. Several other hormones have androgenic (male hormone) effects, including some of the precursors to testosterone, but they pale in comparison with testosterone.

How Fertilization Happens

The Male Part

The male hormones mentioned above are crucial to normal development of sperm in the testicles. There, during their sixty- to ninety-day development in the testes, sperm mature. Notice the epididymis, the first collection area for sperm. The sperm move from the testicle and epididymis through the vas deferens (one per testicle) to the storage tanks, the seminal vesicles. During arousal, a valvelike mechanism turns off the bladder and opens the pathway that allows semen, the sperm-containing fluid, to flow into the urethra through ejaculation.

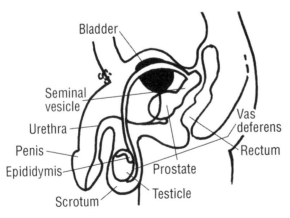

Once sperm are forcefully ejaculated from the penis into the vagina (or onto the moist tissue near it), they can start their Olympic swimming competition. Their tails propel the sperm, and on average, they advance about eight inches per hour.[6] Sperm certainly swim fast enough to get the job done, as the world's current population of about six billion people would suggest. The total distance sperm must travel is only about a hand's length, a journey that requires sperm to travel up the uterus and down the tubes.

If ejaculation occurs within the vagina, sperm immediately encounter cervical mucus, which, if the wife is near her fertile time, is quite receptive.

The Female Part

While the male contribution in human reproduction is sperm, the female contribution is an egg. Egg production is considerably more complex than sperm production, requiring a precise synchrony of brain-regulated hormones. The pituitary gland releases messenger hormones to stir the ovary into action.

Each month in response to a variety of hormonal messages, the ovary develops an egg within a fluid-filled cyst, called a follicle. The follicle releases the egg at ovulation, and ordinarily the egg makes its journey down the fallopian tube. Fertilization generally takes place in the outer one-third of the fallopian tube. Then the embryo travels toward the uterus. Meanwhile, other hormones prepare the uterus to receive a fertilized egg.

No one knows for sure how sperm find the egg, but studies suggest that the egg "woos" sperm with a chemical attraction. Some find the evidence more compelling for a temperature draw—that is, an

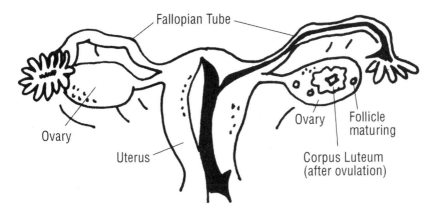

elevated temperature on the side of the female reproductive tract where the egg is. Or perhaps even a "hot egg" itself draws the sperm.[7] Others think lucky sperm randomly stumble on the egg. Proponents of this theory note that 90 percent of sperm are lost in the vagina. The surviving 10 percent, they believe, swim aimlessly, and—as the old joke goes—"demonstrate that men get an early start in hating to stop and ask for directions."

When sperm and egg fail to meet in a given menstrual cycle, a woman starts her period, the body's way of flushing out the preparation material in the uterus.

The Fertilization Event

With the advent of contraceptive methods and reproductive technologies, questions about the origins of human life, personhood, and the sanctity of human life have taken on even greater significance than in the past. The fact that some contraceptive methods prevent a developing embryo from implanting in the uterus raises serious moral and ethical issues. And while Christians have varying views on the purpose of sex, we find much greater agreement about the sanctity of human life at the one-cell stage.

Science has determined that human life begins when egg and sperm unite, DNA aligns, and the resulting being begins to function as a coordinated organism. This event we call *syngamy*. Syngamy happens within twenty-four hours of the moment a single sperm penetrates the egg—the moment of fertilization.

Theologically, life begins at the moment a human has a soul. Most Protestants believe that both the material (physical) and immaterial (spiritual) elements of humanity are transmitted through sexual reproduction, rather than these elements being transmitted in two distinct moments—physical creation and a later ensoulment. Thus, it is believed that children inherit immaterial as well as material traits from their parents.[8] While God did breathe life into the first human after he was formed from the dust, there was no parallel ensoulment event in the woman's creation. We believe that assuming a later time of ensoulment based on a purely arbitrary timeline, and treating the fertilized egg as less than human as a result, oversteps the boundaries of dominion that God has given to humans.[9] That being the case, human life, with all the rights of personhood, begins at syngamy.

An understanding of when life begins is important when we discuss contraception, as some methods are said to work by preventing an already conceived embryo from surviving.

How Contraception Works

Whether you believe reproduction is the primary purpose or an important part of marriage, most people agree that procreation was God's idea, and it's a beautiful design. The world may have strayed far from God's intention in the original plan—that sex should happen between married people and that children should be born within the context of family—but we can still see the fingerprints of our infinitely wise, intelligent Creator in the design.

When we look at how God made human anatomy, how sex works, and how reproduction happens, we marvel at the complex design. And having studied this design, researchers have created a variety of methods to harness or block the natural processes. One approach (barrier methods) works by blocking sperm from reaching the cervical mucus. Other methods block the openings to the fallopian tubes, preventing sperm from getting to the egg. Still others work by killing the sperm. Such spermicides may be used alone but are often used along with barrier methods. Another approach is to disrupt a woman's hormonal cycle to prevent ovulation. And scientists are currently working to develop a male contraceptive that alters sperm production. All of these methods of contraception are temporary measures.

Then there's the surgical route, which provides "permanent" options. For the male, there's vasectomy, which prevents sperm from reaching the ejaculate. Following vasectomy (which requires several weeks after surgery to deplete already stored sperm), the sensations of sexual functioning feel the same, but the results are different. No sperm are released. For the female, there's tubal ligation, which involves closing the fallopian tubes, thus preventing sperm from getting to the egg within the tube. In later chapters, we will explore these options in detail.

LET'S TALK ABOUT IT

1. Based on what you've read, what would you say is God's attitude about sex?
2. Why do you think evangelical women have the highest rates of sexual satisfaction? Has your own experience matched the research?
3. On a scale of one to ten, how important is sex to you? How would your spouse answer that question?
4. Do you feel contraception negatively or positively impacts the sexual experience? Why?
5. If you are choosing to use contraception, what are your reasons for doing so? Are you satisfied that they are good reasons?

PART 2

CONTRACEPTION

OPTIONS, RISKS, AND CHOICES

Chapter 5

Planned Periodic Abstinence

A couple's choice of birth control is a private matter. If we choose to use natural family planning, that's our choice. Couples who use natural family planning should not be the objects of condescension. It's not that we lack education about reproduction; we merely have found a natural way to achieve the ends we desire.

My wife and I practice natural family planning and we hear all the objections. Just because it is sometimes difficult to abstain from sex doesn't mean natural family planning is unreliable. Yet because only four percent of us in the population practice it, it is thought to be strange.

Natural family planning (NFP) is a method of preventing pregnancy that involves abstaining from sexual intercourse during the period of ovulation, which is determined through observation and measurement of the woman's bodily symptoms. Those who practice NFP are often objects of ridicule. People joke, "Do you want to know what we call couples who use natural family planning? We call them 'parents.'"

Yet the truth is that when practiced properly and using the most effective means of observation, NFP has many benefits, including effective child spacing and deepened communication about intimate issues. Many couples who use NFP do so as a result of giving serious thought to honoring God in their private lives—something all couples are wise to consider.

Some advocates of NFP describe it as a lifestyle, insisting that it is not a contraceptive technique or birth control approach, though the desire to avoid having children and the result may be the same as for those who use contraceptives. While it has much to commend it, NFP is natural only in that it involves using no artificial substances—no hormones, barriers, or chemicals.

When it comes to human reproduction, "nothing artificial" means different things to different people. For some, it means using nothing to prevent conception, including periodic abstinence. Many people in this category base their decision on a belief that even abstinence demonstrates a lack of faith, as it suggests an attitude that rejects God's gift of children. For others, "nothing artificial" means not using barriers, chemicals, or hormones but allows meticulously observing the wife's menstrual cycle and abstaining from intercourse during specific times of the month to prevent pregnancy.

This latter group practice what is called natural family planning (NFP). What follows will address the needs of this group. Clearly, NFP requires a lot of discipline. It requires both vigilance in observing female physiology and abstinence during the wife's peak hormonal time, when her interest in sex may often be strongest. And for couples who believe sexual pleasure may be given and received through manual sex, the hormonal desire for satisfaction can be fully met. (Some use NFP in conjunction with barrier techniques during the fertile window.)

The first question couples considering NFP must ask is whether both spouses are committed to the process. For optimal results, it is imperative that both husband and wife take full responsibility for the process. The second question is which of the NFP practices to follow. We will now examine the various NFP practices, moving from the least to the most effective methods.

Withdrawal, Onanism, or the "Amtrak" Method

My husband and I conceived our son via the withdrawal method. We had already had two children, and we used this form of birth control between the first two. (For two and a half years it worked great.) But yes, it can happen. I cried and cried when I found out. I believe children are a blessing from God, but I was going to school and had gotten rid of all of my baby things, as we were done having children. I can't imagine my life now without my son.

Withdrawal, or *coitus interuptus*, is often included in natural family planning techniques. Sometimes it is called the "Amtrak" method because it requires "pulling out of the station just in time." This technique requires withdrawing the erect penis from the vagina just before the man ejaculates. Theoretically, the semen never enters the vagina and cannot reach the egg. Realistically, though, as previously discussed, significant numbers of sperm are released in the pre-ejaculatory fluid of most men, making this so-called technique flawed from the start.

The only thing "natural" about interrupting the sexual response cycle at the exact moment when a man and wife, by exquisite design, yearn for oneness is that it doesn't require the use of any external "helps." Yet because coitus interruptus requires no barriers, chemicals, or hormones, we include it as a method of natural family planning.

Doesn't the Bible condemn this method? Many people believe it does. The story of Onan, in Genesis 38, describes a man using coitus interruptus—hence the name "onanism." And because God killed Onan for his action, many people think withdrawal itself is a sin. Yet as the story reveals, Onan's sin was his failure to fulfill a law that required providing offspring for his dead brother.

Under Old Testament law, when brothers lived together and one died without leaving an heir, another brother was to fulfill the law of the levirate, or the law of the brother-in-law. He did so by taking the widow as his wife and providing an heir to his brother (see Deut. 25:5). In Onan's case, he had sex with his sister-in-law (which he was supposed to do), but he withdrew before ejaculating. In doing so, he intentionally avoided providing an heir, probably because it would diminish his own inheritance. Scripture remains silent about using withdrawal for family spacing, as was practiced by many people of that time. We read only what God thought of Onan's flagrant deceit and disobedience.

While sometimes effective, withdrawal is the most unreliable approach to avoiding pregnancy. With no barriers to block access to the cervix and no chemicals present to kill sperm, the sperm present in the pre-ejaculatory fluid find clear sailing all the way to the awaiting egg.

The Calendar Method

The calendar method, also called the rhythm method, involves charting the wife's usual cycle length and blocking out on the calendar the days when fertility is most likely. This method, effective about 80 percent of the time when faithfully followed, assumes the wife has a regular, predictable period.

Ovulation typically occurs twelve to fourteen days before the onset of the next menstrual cycle, marked by the first day of bleeding. Because cycles vary in length, the fertile time may shift. Thus, with the calendar method, the only way to know when ovulation has occurred is after the period arrives, by counting back twelve to fourteen days.

Unfortunately, most women don't cycle as predictably as clockwork. Stress and illness can alter hormones, resulting in ovulation earlier or later than anticipated. When this happens, ovulation may actually occur on a "safe zone" day—a day when the couple assumed they could have intercourse without conceiving.

For women who have predictable menstrual cycles, the calendar method is more effective in preventing pregnancy than withdrawal is. But for women who ovulate and menstruate in an irregular pattern, the calendar approach is ineffective.

Breastfeeding

I conceived my second child while nursing my first baby.

I'm the mother of two girls, and I am now pregnant with my third, conceived while nursing.

Some people wrongly assume that lactation provides insurance against conceiving again. A new mom may even extend the length of time she breastfeeds for contraceptive effect. Yet while most women who breastfeed around the clock don't ovulate, "most women" isn't the same as "all women." And the time when a woman first ovulates after giving birth varies significantly from woman to woman. One patient of mine (Dr. Bill's) who was nursing her baby had a positive pregnancy test when she came in for an eight-week postpartum checkup.

Most lactating women don't ovulate. In addition, their estrogen levels are low, resulting in decreased libido. They may even find sex painful because the vaginal tissues don't stretch or lubricate normally. Once ovulation resumes, the wife will usually note a positive change in mucus discharge and vaginal comfort during sex. These changes, however, may also go unnoticed.

The effectiveness of breastfeeding as a method of family planning (a method used all over the world) depends on the frequency of nursing and the absence of menstrual flow. Vaginal bleeding suggests resumption of ovulation. As the number of feedings decreases, hormones change, and ovulation is more likely. Proponents of this approach recommend ten or more feedings per day, with no food supplementation for the baby. Quick calculation reveals that satisfying the demands of this technique requires quite a commitment.

Contraception That Requires Looking for Signs

A variety of additional approaches fall under the umbrella of NFP. Each of these approaches requires careful observation of the female cycle, so perhaps "physiological family planning" would be a more accurate label. NFP requires a good understanding of the female hormonal response. When tracked diligently, hormone levels can be used to predict a woman's fertile times. What the couple will do with that information varies. Some, knowing the wife is ovulating, choose to attempt conception. Others choose abstinence. Others choose to use barrier and/or chemical methods during the wife's fertile times.

Ovulation occurs due to gradually increasing estrogen production from the follicle that holds the ovum, or egg. Every fertile woman forms at least one follicle cyst containing a maturing egg during every fertile cycle. The egg is released at ovulation and lives for twelve to twenty-four hours. It can be fertilized only during this rather small window of time. And the increasing estrogen that is produced to prepare the egg for release has other effects on the woman as well. The most notable is the gradual increase in the amount and slickness of her cervical mucus (the fluid from the cervix), which provides a more hospitable environment for sperm to enter the uterus.

To summarize, the "fertile window," during which the egg can be fertilized, lasts twelve to twenty-four hours following ovulation. Yet to calculate the fertile window for the purposes of NFP, we take into consideration the fact that sperm can live for several days. So this window includes the three to five days *before* ovulation as well as the day of and the day after ovulation—about seven days total.

The Ovulation Method

Abstinence makes the heart grow fonder.

I can't imagine having sex without having all of him—receiving his semen.

The ovulation method of natural family planning, also known as the Billings method, was first described by Drs. John and Lyn Billings of Australia. It involves having the wife check her cervical mucus daily, watching for a change. She must do so each time she uses the restroom, obtaining mucus on the toilet tissue or with her fingers. To check the mucus, she takes a small amount of the vaginal discharge between her thumb and forefinger and then gently separates her fingers to see the amount of stretch in the mucus and to feel the degree of slickness. During her most fertile time, a woman's mucus will stretch to an inch or more. It will also be clear, or transparent.

After ovulation, when the hormone progesterone rises, the amount of mucus decreases and becomes cloudy. It loses its stretch as well. For many women, the vagina becomes relatively dry, making it more difficult to obtain mucus. This is the infertile, or "safe," time, during which couples wanting to avoid pregnancy can have unprotected intercourse.

Couples employing the Billings method will use some type of journal or calendar. Some websites supply these materials (see the resources section, under "Abstinence, Periodic Scheduled"), and software programs are available for desktop and handheld devices. The journal serves as a record of mucus days, dry days, and days when blood is present. Certain rules apply about when intercourse is advisable, depending on whether the goal is conception or contraception.

In normally cycling women, the mucus change is noticeable and provides accurate evidence for identifying the fertile time. Women with less regular cycles will still have mucus changes that appear before ovulation, but these women must be diligent in checking daily for such changes.

Highly committed couples find this approach effective, and many couples say it strengthens the marriage because of the shared commitment and responsibility that is necessary in this approach.

The ability to recognize peak cervical mucus is critical to the Billings method. The menstrual cycle revolves around ovulation as hormones build to egg release and then prepare the uterine lining for the implantation of a pregnancy. Afterward the uterine lining sloughs off, evidenced by the menstrual flow. A woman's menstrual tissue consists of more than just blood. A woman's menstrual flow consists of both blood and this tissue lining from within the uterus. A precise balance of hormones allows this uterine lining to slough off without excessive bleeding to allow a new layer to grow for the next cycle.

When hormones are not secreted in the timing and amounts necessary, abnormal bleeding (such as clotting, flooding, or prolonged spotting) occurs. Thus, a woman must be familiar with the usual progression of events. (See chart on p. 60.) When everything happens normally, the most fertile time—the peak time of vaginal discharge—is when the mucus is copious, clear, stretchy, and slippery.

Couples make decisions during each cycle in relation to this peak. The month has prepeak days, peak days, and postpeak days. When it is not clear and slippery, the mucus is considered nonpeak mucus. Thus, a woman can chart her cycles and determine whether there will be sexual contact depending on whether she is at the mucus peak phase.

For this technique to be effective (and when properly used it can have a better than 90 percent success rate in preventing pregnancy), the wife must be diligent about checking and analyzing the cervical

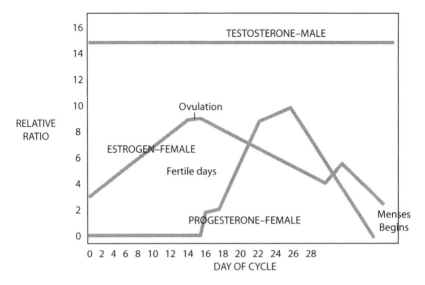

mucus. If she finds mucus on the tissue, she then takes it between her finger and thumb and observes whether it is clear or cloudy, slippery or sticky, stretchy or tacky. She notes these findings in comparison with those of the previous day.

The beginning of the normal cycle is marked by the onset of the menstrual phase. Any bleeding causes alterations in the vaginal discharge, so the presence of blood—even mere spotting—is considered a potentially fertile time because mucus cannot be accurately evaluated.

Prepeak days follow menstruation. On prepeak days, discharge will be scant, and the vagina may feel dry. Then gradually the amount of mucus will increase, and it will begin to feel more slippery and to become clear rather than whitish. In addition, the wife may sense some hormonal nudging toward interest in sexual intimacy. Organized programs offer colored stamps to mark the days on a calendar as a woman develops expertise in the observation process.

Such careful documentation of the physiological changes taking place in a woman's body can be of enormous help to a physician when treating a number of medical problems. With a thorough history of these hormonal changes, a physician can better understand not only cycle regularity and infertility issues but abnormal vaginal discharges, ovarian cysts, early pregnancy, and miscarriage as well.

The Sympto-thermal Method

After ovulation, the ovary secretes the hormone progesterone. As the progesterone level in the bloodstream rises, the hormone causes two changes we must consider for their impact on contraception. Soon after ovulation, a woman's basal temperature rises several tenths of a degree. Her mucus will also change as described in the previous section. These clues provide good evidence that ovulation has occurred.

The progesterone-related rise in the basal body temperature can be useful when monitoring the menstrual cycle. A woman using the sympto-thermal method (sometimes also called the mucothermal method or the temperature charting method) must take her temperature regularly, preferably at the same time every morning. Ideally, she does so before getting up and being active, which elevates the temperature. Because the change in temperature is measured in tenths of a degree, this method requires a great deal of precision. A digital thermometer is recommended. The results are then graphed on a chart (see figure on p. 62).

Some couples add the sympto-thermal method to the Billings method to monitor the woman's cycle. The chart should show a biphasic pattern, meaning that in a normal cycle, the plotted temperatures will have roughly two parts. The temperature remains lower during the first half of the cycle (often 97.2 to 97.4 degrees F), and then at or shortly after ovulation, the temperature gradually rises about half a degree (97.7 to 97.9 degrees F or slightly higher). It remains elevated for the next twelve to fourteen days in a normal, fertile cycle. In fact, when it stays elevated for seventeen or more days in the absence of illness or other hormones (such as those taken by some patients in fertility treatment), pregnancy is likely to have occurred. Progesterone production continues and increases with early pregnancy.

All these observations allow a couple either to avoid or to attempt pregnancy by abstaining or having intercourse during the fertile mucus days. Those using natural family planning to avoid conception should follow these guidelines:

1. Avoid sexual contact during the menstrual flow. Depending on a woman's cycle length, ovulation can take place at the

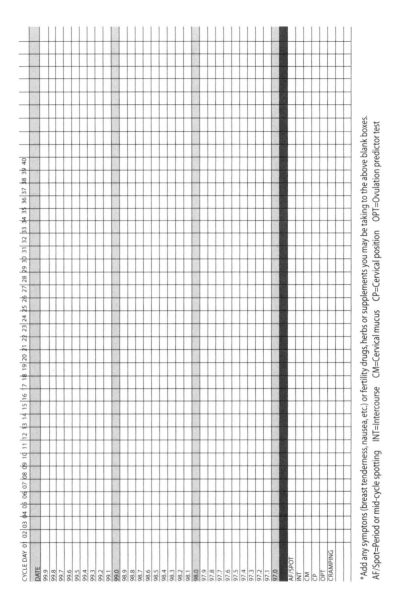

end of menses. Also, some women have spotting at the time of ovulation—the most fertile time.

2. Avoid sex during the prepeak mucus days, the peak day, and the three days following the peak day.

3. The dry days before the beginning of the prepeak mucus are available for sexual contact.

4. Four days after the peak mucus days (peak mucus days are all days during which there is increased mucus) until the onset of menses are nonfertile days.
5. As a woman gains experience with the method and has a good idea of the length of her normal cycles, the dry days at the very end of the menstrual flow can be considered safe.
6. When findings are confusing, assume it is a fertile day and avoid sexual contact or use contraception.

Checking the Cervix

For women who are comfortable inserting a finger into the vagina, additional clues about the timing of the fertile window are available. The position of the cervix and the diameter of the cervical os (the small opening in the middle of the cervix that allows the sperm in and the menses out) provide additional information. The cervical os opens slightly as the fertile window approaches, and the cervical position makes it easier to feel as well.

Few of my patients were interested in regularly inserting a finger up into the vagina to learn these subtleties, and many women were unwilling to become experts in vaginal discharge and cervical mucus. Yet when I presented the same information in the former Soviet Union, listeners were much more interested, motivated by their limited access to other contraceptive techniques. Clearly, the availability or unavailability of contraceptive options affects one's perspective and degree of motivation.

Couples using NFP should keep in mind that seminal fluid can confuse the evaluation of discharge. On the morning after intercourse, the discharge may be moister solely because of the leftover semen. Continue to monitor the discharge throughout the day, and the findings will become more reliable. Some couples limit intercourse to every other day even during the safe periods to ensure an accurate assessment of the mucus. All these factors together—observing mucus changes, noting cervical changes, and charting one's temperature—can give tremendous insight into the time of peak fertility.

Hormone Tests

Some new options are available or are currently being tested that take advantage of these hormone changes. Ovulation is triggered by a hormone surge from the pituitary gland. This hormone, luteinizing hormone (LH), can be detected in the wife's urine twenty-four hours before ovulation. The longevity of the sperm might make this a problem, however, as the news of imminent ovulation may come too late. A fertility computer, now available for several hundred dollars, will track the days and results of urine tests to detect the LH surge. The couple can then abstain during the days before and following ovulation, roughly a total of eight days.

This method is quite effective, though it requires the device (several hundred dollars) and test strips (a few dollars per day during the suspected fertile time), which results in monthly expenditures.

Ovulook

Another approach now on the market is TCI Optics' saliva test kit called Ovulook. It involves checking the estrogen content of a woman's saliva rather than monitoring the cervical mucus. Many women find this method more desirable than regular vaginal checks.

This device is so easy, anyone can use it. When I wake up in the morning, I take my toothbrush and get a saliva sample for the microscope lens. It is great to know when I ovulate.

My husband and I prefer the most natural methods possible to avoid an unplanned pregnancy. I recently obtained Ovulook to help me conveniently and naturally determine when I am fertile. After examining my saliva, I saw tiny ferns and determined I was fertile at a time that I would not have suspected it. Because my fertility is significantly high, my husband is confident that using the Ovulook has kept us from an unplanned pregnancy.

With Ovulook, I can still avoid using artificial means of preventing pregnancy, but now I no longer have to do vaginal self-exams.

As the estrogen level in the blood rises, magnification of the wife's dried saliva reveals a leaf-pattern similar to that of the common fern. This "ferning" pattern grows more complex as estrogen increases and essentially disappears after ovulation (see figure on p. 65). Thus, it lets a couple know when a woman's fertile time is approaching, is present, and has past. It takes about seven minutes for saliva to dry.

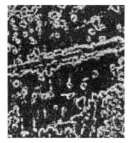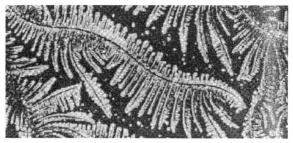

Magnification of the wife's saliva reveals both infertile times (left) and fertile times (right).

Ovulook is a device that helps couples create an ovulation calendar and predict ovulation within a seventy-two-hour window.[1] It requires a one-time purchase (less than seventy-five dollars) of the lipstick-size magnification device. It also requires learning how to read the data, assessing fertile and nonfertile patterns. Salivary test kit manufacturers boast accuracy ratings of about 97 percent, and the kits can be used with fertility computers.

Why Choose NFP?

All of the approaches we have discussed have several clear advantages. First, they're medically safe in that they involve no medications, surgical interventions, foreign objects, or chemicals. They're also either free or inexpensive and are readily available. All are relatively reliable, assuming a great deal of discipline is exercised. If both husband and wife are committed to the process, these methods provide an opportunity for deeper levels of intimacy and mutual understanding through joint decision making about sexual expression.

Couples wanting more personalized direction may contact a trained NFP practitioner, who is certified to assist in teaching couples to effectively use one or more of these techniques.[2] (See the resources section.)

Major studies on NFP performed at Creighton University (Omaha, Nebraska), St. Francis Hospital (Beech Grove, Indiana), and St. Joseph Hospital (Chippewa Falls, Wisconsin) have reported NFP practices are roughly 95 to 97 percent effective in preventing pregnancy. These rates were based on only those couples who have had formal training with NFP counselors.

The success rate may be even higher, approaching 99 percent, with ongoing instruction and diligence in avoiding human error (stretching the rules on occasion). Sexual intimacy between husband and wife is a powerful gift from God, and the desire for union and full expression may cloud the data at times for amorous couples. The basal-body-temperature-charting method, when combined with noting mucus changes, has a success rate of about 85 percent among the general population of those who say they use this method.

Some couples include more subjective symptoms in the mix, including breast tenderness and midcycle pelvic discomfort (so-called *Mittleshmerz*, the ovulatory discomfort that some women can identify). Observing mucus changes alone has a success rate of about 80 percent. While ovulation can be anticipated by mucus changes, one must remember that sperm live for several days; they can survive in favorable mucus long enough to cause pregnancy.

NFP is less effective under some circumstances. Common vaginal infections, including yeast infections, can confuse the mucus-assessment data. And some women have a fairly copious discharge throughout their cycles.

All that having been said, NFP is a good approach, and for those who use it diligently, the success rates both for spacing children and for conceiving are quite good. In addition to respectable success rates, a major advantage of NFP is the ongoing communication between husband and wife that often results from practicing one or more of the NFP methods.

The hard part of the plan is abstaining, and that is what keeps most people from trying it. However, it is during those times that we spend time talking about our priorities. It is those times of abstinence that we talk about whether or not we want to have a child.

This kind of conversation provides portholes to deeper talk and more personal dialogue between us. We've both noticed that with time, open and intimate communication is becoming less a difficulty and more a reflex.[3]

Clearly, couples must make decisions together about family size on a month-by-month, and even a day-by-day, basis. In many cases, the entire responsibility falls on the wife to predict her fertile days.

The husband merely shows up when he gets the green light. Worse yet is when he later blames his wife when pregnancy results, accusing her of deception or incompetence. Husbands and wives need to share the responsibility of determining fertility. Avoiding intercourse on fertile days is the job of both spouses.

NFP: The Christian Solution?

All of the methods described in this chapter, when used to avoid pregnancy, depend on a couple avoiding sexual intercourse for a specific time as determined either by mucus changes, temperature changes, or ferning on the saliva test.

Some people ask whether the premise that a Christian couple can rightfully work to space their children and limit family size is supported biblically since it relies on the practice of periodic abstinence. Under Old Testament law, married couples were instructed to abstain from sexual relations during menstruation and for seven days following. But relations were never prohibited during fertile times. In 1 Corinthians 7:5, Paul sets forth some conditions tempering abstinence between husband and wife. He says abstinence must be (1) by mutual consent, (2) for a specified length of time, and (3) for the purpose of prayer. Why the limitations? First, because of temptation. In this context, Paul presents meeting each other's needs as a purpose for sexual intimacy, apart from childbearing.

Periodic abstinence as a means of avoiding pregnancy does not seem to fit this picture, though certainly the first two conditions are met. That is, the eight to twelve days of abstinence required in each cycle for a specified time and "by mutual consent," which is the strength and heart of these techniques. The third condition, "so that you may devote yourselves to prayer," is not met by NFP. However, in writing to the Corinthian Christians, Paul was not necessarily outlining every case in which abstinence was appropriate. What he did do was lay out an underlying principle that sexual intimacy is designed to meet the need for sexual release within a marriage. Couples should take care to consider all the ramifications before embracing NFP. And here's an important consideration: the abstinence window falls precisely during the time when a woman's hormonal balance is most conducive to her sex drive. And Paul's reason for limiting the time of abstinence is because of the temptation that comes from self-control issues.

A married couple whose ethical point of view allows for manual stimulation and release can pleasure each other during the abstinence period. To reduce the temptation risk during days of prescribed abstinence, other couples using a menstrual timing method use barrier techniques during the fertile time and have intercourse as the mood strikes.

Couples should consider one additional factor when weighing the pros and cons of NFP. Some medical researchers have discovered mounting evidence that points toward a much higher miscarriage rate in late implantations. That is, when fertilization occurs at the end of the abstinence window because of a long-surviving egg, the risk of miscarriage in couples using NFP may be higher because of the delay.[4] Does this mean the technique should be avoided because of the possibility of an abortifacient (abortion-inducing) effect? Probably not, as the evidence that an abortion-inducing effect occurs is indirect and preliminary. But it bears further investigation.

We encourage readers to avoid referring to planned abstinence as either "natural" or "biblical." Clearly, it should not be touted as *the* method of family planning that represents faith or truly trusts God, as some argue.

One final word: Often the mere mention of NFP immediately evokes stories about those for whom it failed. Anecdotes abound about those who've had unplanned pregnancies while practicing NFP. Much of this is probably due to lumping all of the physiological observation methods together with the withdrawal method and lactation for contraceptive effect. So we close by dispelling yet another myth—that those who use NFP have many unplanned children and large families. The contraceptive success rates associated with the Billings method and related practices point to the opposite. And many couples opting to use barrier, chemical, and hormonal means of contraception would be wise to understand the marvel of their bodies' natural processes as God created them. Couples can use NFP either in an effort to time a desired pregnancy or to avoid pregnancy. The effectiveness level of NFP puts it in a league with the best barrier methods. It's actually better, if practiced diligently.

And of all methods of contraception, it is the only one of which it can be said that it has absolutely no side effects other than unfulfilled longings.

LET'S TALK ABOUT IT

1. When it comes to contraception, who do you think has primary responsibility? Him? Her? Both?
2. Are you comfortable using "artificial," or external, contraceptive methods, such as hormonal adjustments?
3. Do you prefer approaches that rely on physiology, such as NFP?
4. Are you comfortable with the process of checking cervical mucus, charting basal body temperature, and planning periodic abstinence?
5. How do you think the NFP approach fits with the purpose of sexuality as God designed it?
6. Describe your sexual health and that of your spouse. Is intimacy a uniting, strong, delightful experience? Or is it more of a chore? How might NFP affect your intimate life?

CHAPTER 6

A TRIP TO THE PHARMACY

CHEMICALS AND BARRIERS

Let me get this straight . . . I'm supposed to spend most of the month trying to muster up some interest because my hormones are working against me. Then finally, just when I feel those nudgings toward my drawer full of risqué lingerie, it's time to abstain? People say this is natural. No way. It's unnatural!

I read about all these women who have problems with low desire. I'd have low desire too if I had to suppress my desire at ovulation time and conjure it up when I had PMS.

I am one of those rare guys with a low sex drive. My wife feels neg-lected, unattractive, and unsexy. And wouldn't you know—when I'm finally in the mood, nine times out of ten it's either during her period or during the abstinence time.

Many people like me believe abortion is wrong. But that doesn't mean I'm against birth control. Life begins at conception,* not at ejaculation.

Are inspecting vaginal mucus, checking saliva, touching the cer-vical os, charting your temperature, and abstaining at midcycle every month excluded from your top-ten list of romantic activities? While natural family planning (NFP) is inexpensive, for some

---

*As defined in the glossary of this book.

couples the unifying effect of making these decisions as a couple seems like eating chalk compared to the chocolate mousse of spontaneous, unbridled sexual ardor.

Perhaps you're among the couples who feel this way, and you've decided to use contraception. A tour through your local pharmacy or the pharmacy department at your local grocery store will introduce you to a variety of available contraceptive products.

Perhaps you've never explored this region of the store. Maybe you've turned your eyes away because before marriage, you weren't supposed to know about this stuff. And now that you can know about it, you look forward to such a trip with the same enthusiasm you have for carrying a huge box of tampons to the teenage boy at the checkout stand. What follows is a chance to find out what's there without having to leave home.

The Condom for Him

One famous condom brand is Ramses. But frankly, I wonder about the effectiveness of a condom named after a pharaoh who had over one hundred wives and over two hundred kids.

Even if you've tried not to, you've probably already seen the condom selection, or the "rubber rack," as it is sometimes labeled by hip teens. It's hard to miss because most pharmacies strategically locate these aids adjacent to the pharmacist's counter. This probably has less to do with boosting point-of-sale volumes and more with teen shoplifters boosting products because they're too embarrassed or too young to ask for them.

Three thousand years ago, an amorous Egyptian couple experimented with a linen pouch, producing the world's first known condom.[1] Always relatively inexpensive and readily available, the male prophylactic has been around for centuries. Inventive couples have employed a remarkable variety of household items as barriers, but the animal intestine condom wins the prize for staying power through the generations, being the barrier of choice until the invention of rubber and the refinement of latex. Today's condoms are usually made of latex rubber. Correct usage requires consistent use, with the condom placed over the *erect* penis *before* it makes vaginal contact. Remember, small amounts of sperm are often found in the pre-ejaculate, the tiny amount of fluid that exudes from the penis before the sensation of ejaculation. Starting to have sex without the condom and then stopping to put it on often results in unintended pregnancy.

Pharmacists recount tales of condom requests from young men who ask for *extra* large. Apparently the young men don't realize that, unlike shoes, the generally available mass-produced condom is "one size fits all." So much for endless e-mail ads about increasing penis size. (It *is* possible to surgically increase penile length and circumference somewhat, but not to the point that a condom extender would be required.)

My own *tour de pharmacie*, done as "field research" for this book, yielded remarkable treasures. Past the assorted douches and personal lubricants, I found an array of over-the-counter contraceptive products. Among them sat displays with an astonishing variety of condoms including creative brand names with alluring labels promising "assorted colors," "luscious flavors," and "ribs and bumps for mutual pleasure." There were garden-variety latex condoms, non-latex condoms for those with allergies, and lambskin condoms for those who prefer the "natural, biological" approach to barrier contraception. They came in "microsheer" and "ultrathin," with large reservoir tips, even in a "large" for the confident male. (While the one-size-fits-all dictum is correct, some companies market a large size for the male with an ego to match his condom product.)

Some products included spermicidal lubrication, but most did not. Others were treated with a "desensitizing chemical"—a local anesthetic that can make the penis less sensitive to tactile sensations and thus enable the male to prolong intercourse before ejaculation. It may give the premature ejaculator enough confidence to last longer.

Prices ranged from about twenty-five cents per condom for latex to a dollar for the nonlatex, and up to two bucks apiece for the lambskin. The basic idea behind condoms is to keep sperm out of the vagina, thus preventing them from making the quest for the egg, which could result in fertilization. The average male ejaculation is propelled from the body at 28 miles per hour—roughly the speed of Mr. Cannonball at the circus, propelled across the big top into the net. So the challenge is to make a product that's thin enough for pleasure but thick enough to stop an explosion of speeding swimmers. So far it looks like mission accomplished.

Condoms are effective with proper, consistent usage. (Inconsistent usage is the big problem with teen sex, but this book is for married people.) This means using condoms properly *every single time*, unless you are also using natural family planning or another ovulation monitoring method to pinpoint fertile times. The condom provides excellent protection against pregnancy unless it breaks or leaks. Statistics show a 3 to 12 percent pregnancy rate per year with typical use. The condom is also currently the best barrier method for preventing some sexually transmitted infections, although the media has overstated its effectiveness. The national "Safe Sex" program, pushing condom use for protection against STIs (sexually transmitted infections), was less effective than anticipated, not so much because of condom failure but because sexually active people did not use the condoms consistently and correctly. This resulted in pregnancies and infections with STIs.

The Male Condom

Many married couples have successfully used condoms for spacing their children. The most common complaint is "having to stop in the middle of everything" to put on the condom. There's no way around this, though it does help to keep a condom ready by the bed at all times, rather than leaving it stashed in a bathroom drawer. Putting it on as part of the process of foreplay can lower the frustration level. Those who leave condoms in their glove compartments or wallets, however, may find that the deterioration due to aging and exposure to extreme temperatures make them more liable to rupture.

Condoms allow the husband to participate actively in the contraception process. The condom is currently the only temporary contraceptive available for male use. As the perceptive reader will have noted, all other contraceptive approaches (with the exception of withdrawal and vasectomy) are targeted at the female. Scientists are working to develop methods that inhibit sperm production, but to date nothing effective enough for recommendation is available in the U.S. market. (We will discuss this in some detail in chapter 12.)

Couples often use a spermicide in addition to condoms for protection against spills and ruptures. But some spermicides can dissolve latex, so it's important to check for compatibility. Couples using spermicides may also experience burning, itching, redness, or inflammation. The condom's latex, its lubricant, and the spermicide can all cause allergic reactions. The only way to treat such symptoms is to change brands.

Some guys consider condoms just plain sexy. And many men and women like condoms because they sometimes make erections last longer. There are some disadvantages, though. A common complaint is that condoms decrease the level of pleasurable sensation.

In addition, a couple that has just enjoyed an intensely powerful sexual connection may feel a sense of abandonment afterward if they're unable to lie wrapped in each other's arms enjoying the afterglow. Correct usage requires fairly rapid withdrawal of the erect penis from the vagina to keep the semen in the condom reservoir.

The World Health Organization estimates that the pregnancy rate for condoms—when used correctly during every act of intercourse—is 3 percent at twelve months. This means a couple using only a condom, and using it correctly, has a 3 percent chance of becoming pregnant in a year. This includes pregnancy due to condom breakage. But the pregnancy rate for actual (imperfect) use can be much higher—10 to 14 percent. This is because people use the condom either inconsistently or incorrectly, not because the device has slipped or broken during intercourse.[2]

The Condom: For Her

That's what it takes for him. What about for her? Women have been using barrier contraceptives for more than three thousand years. Ancient Egyptians, Greeks, and Romans inserted a mixture of herbs, tree resins, and honey or oil into their vaginas. Some African women used hollowed out okra pods as a vaginal pouch, somewhat like the modern female condom. Roman women used goat bladders in a similar manner (while their partners used various forms of animal membrane as sheaths for the penis).[3] Today's women have some superior options.

As we continue our pharmacy tour, in the next aisle over, we find the female counterpart of the male condom. There is less variety here, as the female condom has never caught on in the United States.

Yeah, we tried using a female condom. Once. It was like having a romantic encounter with a Glad Zip Lock Bag.

My first glance at this plastic monstrosity made me wonder how all that would fit inside.

My husband and I take turns. One time we use a male condom; the next time we use a female condom. It seems better than having all the responsibility fall on just one of us.

I didn't know whether to insert it or wrap a fish in it and put it in the freezer.

Picture a plastic bag shaped like a cylinder that's open at one end, and you have a general idea of what the female condom looks like. It's a pouch made of clear plastic, with rings at both ends. The sealed end with a ring holding the pouch open is inserted into the vagina, forming a barrel-shaped bag with an open ring at the outside of the vagina, permitting entry of the penis. Intercourse takes place inside the pouch. The ejaculate is captured within the pouch so it never reaches the cervical mucus. These pouches are more resilient and thicker than most male condoms and rarely, if ever, rupture during correct usage. Nevertheless, the female condom is

Plastic sheath with ring at both ends

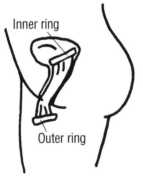

Inner ring

Outer ring

How to grasp
female condom
for insertion

slightly less effective in pregnancy prevention than the male condom (it has a looser fit). Cost runs about a dollar fifty to two bucks per condom.

Only water-based lubricants should be used with the male and the female condoms. Also, the male and female condoms were not designed to be used together. The friction can cause either condom to bunch up or tear.

Female condoms do provide some protection against STIs such as herpes and HPV (venereal wart) infections. Unfortunately, research data indicates that if one partner has an STI and the couple stays married for a number of years, the odds are high that the noninfected spouse will eventually contract the STI.

According to the manufacturer of the female condom, 40 to 60 percent of those who try it continue its use, but that means 40 to 60 percent also discontinue its use. When surveyed, those who continued said they found it more pleasurable than the male condom. The female device is less constricting and can be inserted up to eight hours before intercourse, so insertion doesn't spoil the mood.

Chemical Warfare: Weapons of Mass Sperm Destruction

As we continue our tour, we find the chemical arsenal next to the condom rack. Chemical approaches to contraception come in many forms but center on the spermicidal activity of a compound called nonoxynol-9, which is about 70 to 85 percent effective in preventing conception. No, it's not a detergent. It's a spermicide that has been on the market for years and is used in various types of products. Delivery systems include a bullet-shaped vaginal suppository and a contraceptive gel that can be used by itself or with a condom. Be certain that any chemical contraceptive you consider using along with condoms is labeled as approved for this purpose.

Delfen makes a contraceptive foam that's injected into the vagina, again using nonoxynol as the spermicidal agent. There are other brands of contraceptive foam, and one manufacturer markets nonoxynol as a contraceptive film. A thin material is inserted well up into the vagina where it melts and liquefies, coating the cervix with the spermicidal gel—same spermicide, different method. Some women find this is a more pleasant way to apply the spermicide.

Costs range from roughly one dollar per contraceptive film to about ten dollars for a multiple-use package of gel or foam. Price per application varies between products. One of the most common complaints about foams and films is that they taste unpleasant and can thus interfere with oral pleasuring.

This is just a sampling of the many products available over the counter. You can order condoms online, but if you happen to run out, it can be a long wait. If you need to buy contraceptives at your local drugstore, don't be shy. Shop like a hunter. Go in the store, grab what you want, and pay confidently. If you do that, no one will give it a second thought. The main thing: don't let 'em see you sweat, or they'll *know* you don't know what you're doing, and they might think you're not married. (Of course, you can always wave your ring.)

The Sponge

In a 1995 episode of *Seinfeld*, Elaine's character scours New York for pharmacies that carry her favorite birth control method—the sponge. Eventually she finds and buys an entire case. Having only twelve boxes left, she hoards her supply, making it last by raising her pitifully low standards. That is, she puts potential lovers through extensive interviews to determine if they're "sponge worthy."

The Today Sponge

While Elaine's story is fictional, and we certainly don't endorse her character's promiscuity, plenty of real women did buy up all the sponges they could find that year because the sponge was taken off the U.S. market. It was a popular contraceptive method, but its maker ran into some problems with its manufacture and quality control.

I used the Today Sponge for years in my early relationship with my husband. We loved it! It was both convenient and reliable. I think it's one of the greatest modern forms of contraception.

As mentioned in the chapter on myths, women throughout history have tried a variety of methods for preventing pregnancy. Some of the earliest barrier methods go back some five thousand years, to the time when people moistened sea sponges with diluted lemon juice and inserted them into the vagina, both to block and absorb semen. Women experimented with the sea-sponge concept, soaking it in different substances with potential sperm-weakening effects, such as olive oil, vinegar, and even brandy.

In the 1700s, inhabitants of the Mediterranean region preferred lemon juice. In fact, Casanova himself is said to have advocated the use of half a peeled lemon as a forerunner to today's contraceptive sponge. Forty years ago, a physician in Australia reported in his medical text that "Soaking a sponge in diluted lemon juice and using it as a vaginal tampon is theoretically not surpassed in reliability by any modern clinical contraceptive."[4] So much for progress.

The modern sponge, made of polyurethane foam, is an inch-thick doughnut-shaped device that is about the size of a flattened Ping-Pong ball. It also has a ribbon attached, which the patient can grasp when removing the sponge. Many people imagine it works by a barrier effect, but the sponge doesn't block the sperm from reaching the cervical opening; it is not truly a barrier method. The sponge's primary mode of action is that it contains a spermicide— you guessed it—nonoxynol-9, the same ingredient found in the other chemical contraceptives. The sponge releases this spermicide over a twenty-four-hour period.

The woman using a sponge should, after washing her hands, follow the instructions on the package. It is inserted before intercourse and is effective for up to twenty-four hours, even with multiple encounters. However, it must remain in place for at least six hours after penetration to work effectively as a contraceptive. It should be removed within twenty-four hours for good hygiene. Unlike the diaphragm (described below), the sponge is designed to be available over the counter, comes in one-size-fits-all, and is disposable.

Other than occasional infections (including toxic shock, caused by patients forgetting and leaving tampons or sponges inserted too long), the sponge is fairly effective and convenient.

Today the sponge has been reintroduced for sale in Canada, and a U.S. company has bought the rights to sell it in the states. At the time of this writing, it is pending final FDA approval.

Ever since I got the email saying they'd be shipped, I've been singing that Aretha Franklin song, "Freedom, freedom."

One writer, delighted at the prospect of the sponge's return, told what she saw as its primary benefits: "Maybe it's laziness but I like the convenience of it, not having to go to the doctor to get a prescription or a shot. And I don't like the idea of polluting my body with all those hormones."[5]

When the sponge returns to the market, it will probably have the same effectiveness rating as before—about 84 to 91 percent.[6] It appears to work less effectively for women who have been pregnant.

Barrier Methods Requiring a Doctor's Assistance

Having completed our trip to the pharmacy, we will now head to the doctor's office. There we'll survey the cabinets for some devices that are unavailable at the drugstore—devices that require a doctor's assistance.

The Diaphragm

My husband likes the diaphragm very much. He jokes around, calling it a hat, and tells his friends that he will never go out without putting on a hat.

One thing led to another, and I found myself saying, "Wait, I have to put in my diaphragm!" Once I take out my contact lenses, I can barely find my way around. I stumbled, naked, from the bedroom to the bathroom, couldn't find the light switch, and rifled blindly through my things until I found my diaphragm. While I was applying lubricating gel, the diaphragm sprang out of my hands, forcing me to crawl around trying to locate it by feel. At this point he, wondering where on earth I was, came to the door and switched on the light. These days, to no surprise, I'm back on the pill.

It took me an hour practicing in the gyno's office trying to get the @#$%^ diaphragm in and out.

I tried all the other methods. They had unbearable side effects. The diaphragm was a rescuer for me.

Approximately the size of the palm of the hand, the diaphragm is a round latex "hat" that a woman places over her cervix. Diaphragms come in several sizes, so a woman planning to use one must see her doctor or nurse practitioner for fitting. The cost of this contraceptive is the cost of the medical office visit and of the diaphragm itself, which is usually twenty to thirty dollars (including its case), and the ongoing cost of spermicidal gel. Unfortunately, clever sperm can find their way around the edges of the diaphragm, making chemical warfare necessary in conjunction with the actual barrier. In other words, correct usage requires the application of spermicidal foam or jelly made for diaphragm use. The spermicide is applied inside and around the edges of the diaphragm every time it is inserted.

A frequent complaint about contraceptive methods is that many of them inhibit spontaneity. For this reason, many couples like the diaphragm. The wife can insert it nightly as part of her bedtime routine and she never has to stop and put it in if she and her husband decide they're in the mood.

The diaphragm should remain in place for eight to ten hours after use. Once removed, it should be washed in soap and water and stored in its case. (I had one patient who did not use her case, and her dog gnawed on the diaphragm, severely reducing its potential for effectiveness.) Diaphragm users must reapply the diaphragm gel if more than two hours have elapsed since the time of insertion. Additional gel is recommended for each additional romantic interlude within a twenty-four-hour period. *This does not mean the diaphragm should be removed.* Rather, it should be left in place and spermicidal cream should be inserted directly into the vagina.

To check for rips or tears in the diaphragm before inserting it, hold it up to a light source to see if any pinpoints of light shine through. Next, fill it with water to make sure it doesn't leak. Throw it away if it has tears or leaks. A woman using the diaphragm has about a 5 to 10 percent chance of conceiving in a year. A lot depends on how vigilant she is about using it regularly and correctly.

The Diaphragm

The Cervical Cap

Cervical caps are great. I had one for years. I had no pregnancies, no urinary tract infections, no yeast infections—unlike with the diaphragm, which I had used previously. The cap cost more initially, but I save money in the long run, as it's more durable and you use much less spermicidal jelly.

I've used a cervical cap for years, with no problems whatsoever, so naturally I think it's great. Neat, convenient, and not felt by either partner. On the down side, it is an imported device not prescribed as much as other methods in this country, and the sizes available are limited. So if you don't happen to get a good fit with one of the available sizes, you're out of luck.

I used a cervical cap for almost fifteen years and loved it. It was relatively easy to use and I could keep it in for several days.

Beware. I got pregnant using a cervical cap. The midwife who fitted me for the cap told me after I got pregnant that the effectiveness of a cap is lower for women who have had children—something to do with the cervix having been stretched out and having deeper "wrinkles" in it after childbirth. The cap apparently doesn't seal off as well.

It is hard to get it in at first, but after a while it becomes easy.

A method similar to the diaphragm is the cervical cap. Never very popular in the United States, the cervical cap has been a favorite contraceptive method in Europe since the mid-1800s.[7] It is a latex rubber, thimble-shaped device similar to the diaphragm but

The
Cervical
Cap

smaller. Unlike the diaphragm, which covers the entire roof of the vagina, the cervical cap must be fitted to the cervix itself. It is a bit more rigid and more challenging to get in and out. A woman who uses it must be quite comfortable reaching far into her vagina for insertion and removal. Once the cap is in place, it is hardly felt by either partner.

The cap works as a sperm barrier, providing fairly secure coverage at the cervix. Suction helps keep it in place. Intended for use with a spermicide, the cap can be inserted for up to two days without requiring additional gel. It should remain in place for at least eight hours after intercourse.

The cervical cap's effectiveness is cited as being between 60 and 80 percent. Occasionally caps get "stuck" on the cervix or cause cervical irritation or damage. Leaving a cap in for more than two days can also ulcerate the cervix.

Most women who use the cervical cap are quite happy with it. Because a woman can insert it more than a day before intercourse, it allows for a greater degree of spontaneity than other barrier methods.

While we're at the doctor's office, we will now turn our attention to the most revolutionary of all contraceptive options: the pill. Whether people think it's "the devil's aspirin" or "the greatest thing to happen to women since the right to vote," nearly everyone has an opinion about it.

LET'S TALK ABOUT IT

1. List what you consider to be the greatest pros and cons of using the following contraceptives. Have your spouse do the same. Then compare your answers.
   - Spermicide
   - Male condom
   - Female condom
   - Sponge
   - Cervical cap
   - Diaphragm
   - A combination of these products

2. Which of these contraceptives had the most pros for you? What factors might prevent you from using your favorite method consistently?

CHAPTER 7

WHAT ABOUT THE PILL?

I was thrilled that being on the pill enabled me to shift the time my period was due until after the wedding night and honeymoon.

I don't understand why the pill didn't work. I took one without fail every time I had sex.

I love getting my period on a Sunday, and it's over by Monday night. Also, the flow is light. I used to have six heavy days with horrible cramps and vomiting. The pill cleared that right up.

I'm not too crazy about the idea of taking birth control pills, but since I have acne I've been on Accutane, which can cause horrendous birth defects. So the pill gives me peace of mind.

I am wondering about birth control pills. I suspect they could make the love stronger between my husband and me because we wouldn't have to worry about my getting pregnant.

Does the pill prevent conception? Sure it does—because abstinence is the best way to avoid getting pregnant. Once I went on the pill, I lost all interest in sex.

Mention birth control pills, and you may evoke some strong opinions. You may end up wondering what's true and what's not. For starters, a woman on the pill must take it daily, not "as needed," as described by one of the women above. Also, when people talk about the pill, they're not talking about just *one* kind of pill but about a variety of products. Others bring up ethical concerns. We'll talk about these in the next chapter.

Before we get very far in considering the pros and cons, it's important to understand both how the female body works and how the pill works.

The Female Cycle

The female reproductive system is remarkably complex. In its design and in hormone production, it can be likened to a symphony, in which each instrumentalist must play at the right time, hit the right notes, and hold them for the proper length of time. When everything works as it should, the result is beautiful music. The female reproductive cycle, like a symphony, crescendos monthly at

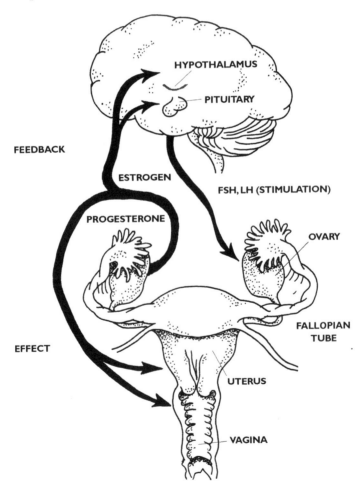

the time of ovulation and reaches its finale with the onset of menstruation. Ovulation is the focus of most female hormonal contraceptive approaches. If ovulation can be blocked, no pregnancy will occur, regardless of when or how often intercourse happens.

If the menstrual cycle is a symphony, the conductor is the pituitary, a tiny gland shaped like a punching bag that extends from a stalk at the brain's base, or underside. The concert begins in a centrally located part of the brain called the hypothalamus, which sends neurochemical messages to the pituitary. In direct response to these messages (stimulation), the pituitary directs like a conductor, "marking the beat" with messenger hormones that include follicle stimulating hormone (FSH) and luteinizing hormone (LH). These hormones must be released throughout the month, providing progressive synchronous bursts, or pulses. The ovaries, thyroid, and other hormone glands respond to the hormonal stimulation, like musicians making music. To summarize, FSH (follicle stimulating hormone)

- stimulates estrogen production
- matures the egg for release
- makes a woman generally happy about the man in her life, thanks to the effects of estrogen

LH (luteinizing hormone)

- works primarily to cause egg release
- causes final preparation of the uterus for implantation via progesterone production
- causes bloating, cramping, and crankiness and can make a woman apathetic or even hostile to the man in her life, due to the effects of progesterone

The production of these two key hormones affect so much of what it means to be a female.

The Eggs

A baby girl is born with thousands of eggs—all she will ever have. At her birth, every one of these eggs is immature. But once she grows into a young woman and begins to menstruate, each month

FSH stimulates a few immature eggs to mature, resulting in the formation of small, fluid-filled sacs called follicle cysts. Eventually one of the maturing eggs becomes dominant. FSH also causes the adjacent cells of the ovary to start producing increasing amounts of estrogen. Ah, estrogen—the key to feminization. In the woman, this key unlocks mysterious emotional qualities and gives her feminine breasts and hips. Give a man enough estrogen, and he'll develop breasts, hips, a higher voice, and a soft face where once he was scruffy (truly a disturbing image).

Estrogen

Estrogen in proper amounts is essential to fertility. Without it, the egg would not mature to ovulation and the uterine lining would be an unfriendly landing zone for the embryo. During the fertile time of a woman's cycle, estrogen gently nudges her toward sexual desire. It also aids pleasurable entry of the penis by providing abundant vaginal fluids that enhance vaginal elasticity. Estrogen is also responsible for making the cervical fluid that is a favorable environment for sperm.

LH

Once FSH has done its job, the pituitary conductor signals to LH, "It's ti-i-i-ime!" This tells the follicle to let go of the ripe egg, triggering ovulation. It also stimulates the production of another powerful hormone—progesterone. (Give a man progesterone, and he'd probably get crampy, cranky, and bloated or want to sleep all afternoon.) Estrogen is still being produced, but progesterone becomes dominant.

The Uterine Lining

During the first part of a woman's normal cycle, estrogen causes the endometrial lining to grow, the uterine landing zone for the potential fertilized egg. Once progesterone takes over in the latter half of the cycle, the lining becomes even friendlier. Its cells make a sugarlike substance in preparation for a pregnancy. If you looked at this lining under a microscope, you would normally see tiny packets of a glycogen sugar, a rich source of energy for the potential developing embryo. If a sperm fertilized an egg in this cycle, the embryo should be well on its way down the tube and headed for the "sweet" uterus.

Progesterone

In addition to making the lining friendly, progesterone also changes the cervical mucus, making it thicker, whiter, and less favorable for sperm. If fertilization hasn't occurred, the egg is no longer viable, so there's no need to let in more sperm.

We can observe the effects of progesterone several ways:

- Using MRI or ultrasound, we can observe the amount and character of the endometrial lining's thickness.
- Looking through a microscope, we can note the disappearance of the ferning pattern in a sample of cervical mucus taken after ovulation.
- Observing the woman's saliva after it dries, we can note the absence of the ferning pattern, which is present until ovulation.

Each of these elements provides clues for ways to alter the menstrual cycle and thus prevent egg release.

The Pituitary

One particularly interesting part of God's design in the female is what we call a "feedback mechanism." When the estrogen level rises, the pituitary gland "hears" a change and turns down the volume on FSH (note the arrows on the diagram in the beginning of this chapter.) Similarly, when the pituitary senses that the blood level of estrogen is sufficient, it is satisfied and stops producing FSH.

Most people have a similar feedback mechanism at work when they get hungry. The brain senses lower blood sugar and registers this lack as hunger, whether or not the stomach is full. So the brain sends powerful messages: "Chocolate! Butterfingers! Cheesecake! Doritos! *Now!*" So we snarf down food, sometimes even before the satiety center can say, "Enough, Tubbo." Soon we feel satisfied (or stuffed), and the hunger pangs disappear.

How Hormonal Contraceptives Work

When it comes to contraception, here's where human intervention comes in. Most hormonal approaches to avoiding pregnancy involve sending a false message to the pituitary, telling it, "I'm satisfied; the job's been done." So the FSH pulses are turned off, and no egg is directed into action.

While this may sound easy, it's actually rather difficult. First, it means the patient's body has to absorb estrogen from a source other than the ovary, namely by taking a pill. The difficulty is in giving the body the precise amount of estrogen that it needs to suppress ovulation yet keep moods normal. Digestive problems can reduce the estrogen level to below what is needed to keep the pituitary from releasing FSH. Also, oral estrogen is processed through the liver, where it's metabolized, released into the blood stream, and ultimately sent to the pituitary to shut it down. But if the liver gets busy due to illness or other medications, the estrogen level may not reach the level needed for the desired result.

Some medications, such as antibiotics, anticonvulsants, and herbal preparations such as Saint-John's-wort, can also alter the estrogen level sufficiently to allow the sleeping conductor—the pituitary—to wake up, take the podium, and start directing the ovaries. Many pregnant women have said, "I was on the pill, but I also took some antibiotics."

Estrogen received by pill, patch, injection, or paste will affect blood estrogen levels and pituitary response. Progesterone, too, given by pill or injection, can affect the pituitary release of LH and the uterine lining. Progesterone given when the lining of the uterus is unprepared has the effect of thinning the lining, so it's less favorable for implantation. (We'll explore this in depth in the next chapter.) Only when the endometrial tissue is primed with estrogen will the progesterone-stimulated uterine lining convert to its lush, sweet environment for the embryo.

Hormonal contraceptive approaches take advantage of the physiological symphony by providing "piped-in music" and thus giving the orchestra members the month off. These piped-in hormones slow the normal growth of the sweetened lining of the uterus, and they make it harder for sperm to swim through the cervical mucus.

Now that we have a general understanding of how things work, we'll consider how the varying options of hormonal contraceptives affect a woman's body.

Combination Oral Contraceptives (COCs)

To some people, the phrase "birth control pill" suggests that birth, rather than fertilization, is what's being prevented. In other words, some people understand from this term that an embryo is created but is then prevented from implanting in the uterus, so it dies—which is not the case. For the sake of these people, we'll use a different designation: combination oral contraceptives (COCs). Why "combination"? Because COCs include a combination of hormones: estrogen and progestin, a synthetic progesterone.

COCs are designed to prevent ovulation. As was mentioned earlier, if naturally produced hormones are the orchestra music, COCs are like piped-in music. When COC hormones are present, the pituitary does not direct via the FSH messages.

Some have likened this process to artificial pregnancy: the pills tell the body, "I'm already pregnant." That's an inaccurate analogy. Hormone levels in a woman taking COCs are nowhere near as high as in a pregnant woman. In fact, since the introduction of hormonal contraceptives, the amount of estrogen included in COCs has steadily declined. Current pills contain roughly one-fifth of the estrogen level of the originals.

Taken properly, and assuming no other confounding variables, COCs effectively block FSH, thus keeping the egg from maturing. One complicating factor is that most women who take a steady, low dose of estrogen alone will have unwanted bleeding, either unpredictable spotting or a heavy flow. Thus, progesterone is added because it stabilizes the uterine lining. The combination of low doses of estrogen and small amounts of progesterone means a patient usually experiences no bleeding except during the pill-free or placebo week. Then she can expect a light menstrual flow.

Progesterone blocks the production of LH that might otherwise trigger ovulation in the unlikely event that an egg was maturing despite the low estrogen level supplied by the pill. Thus, the combination pill has dual effects. It keeps the egg from maturing while minimizing estrogen production from the rest of the ovary, and it prevents the "Time to ovulate!" message. The estrogen level is too low to cause a lush growth of endometrial tissue. And the progesterone results in less favorable cervical mucus, thus impeding the sperm. At least this is the way the pills are *supposed* to work. (We are assuming the patient is taking them exactly as prescribed.)

Pill Options: Mono, Bi, Tri

Combination pills come in various forms. Understanding them is as simple as one, two, three—mono, bi, tri. Some pills are *monophasic*, meaning they contain one combination of hormones that is the same in each of twenty-one active pills. *Biphasic* pills offer a ten-pills-of-one-kind, eleven-of-another approach. These pills include the same amount of estrogen throughout, but the amount of progesterone gradually increases. For the first ten days of the cycle, the woman takes one combination of hormones. Beginning on day eleven, she is taking pills that contain a different combination—generally with more progesterone. This recipe allows pharmaceutical companies to use less total hormone, resulting in fewer side effects.

Triphasic pills consist of three consecutive seven-day sets of pills. Each pill within the set has the same combination of hormones, but the estrogen-progesterone dosages vary in each step.[1] For many women, this means less hormone taken, fewer side effects, and less spotting (light breakthrough bleeding that can go on for days). Triphasic pills remain popular at the time of this writing. Some women, however, prefer the simplicity and effectiveness of the monophasic approach.

How do you know which approach is best for you? Talk with your physician. Considering the multiple combinations of hormonal options, types of packaging, and assorted pharmaceutical companies, the average patient has many options. Generally, a physician will prescribe a low-dose, multiphasic pill for contraception. If significant side effects develop, including no menstrual flow or excessive bleeding, changes can be made to find the best match for the patient. One reason pills are popular is because doctors can usually find a combination that works well with a given woman's metabolism. Still, some patients' bodies can't tolerate hormonal contraception.

One of the more recent oral contraceptive approaches, Seasonale, regulates the body in such a way that the menstrual cycle occurs over three months rather than one month. Researchers are still studying the effects of suppressing menstruation for this length of time, but some women love the idea of menstruating only four times a year. Seasonale involves eighty-four active pills followed by seven inactive pills, or placebos, during which time the woman has her menstrual flow. Because Seasonale is a new approach, we have no studies of long-term side effects resulting from such prolonged menstrual suppression.

Might there be some function in having monthly periods? To our knowledge, no. As sex therapist Laura Berman notes, "Most women are not aware of the fact that with any contraceptive pill, they do not have a (genuine) menstrual period. Their monthly cycle is actually a 'pill-period' or 'withdrawal bleed,' which is not the same as a period."[2]

Others have suggested that women need monthly periods to rid the body of excess stored iron. They are concerned that reducing the number of periods may add to the risk of heart attack and stroke. The theory behind this is that if the blood count gets high, because of increased iron the risk of clotting complications increases and could result in heart attack (caused by tiny clots in the coronaries) or stroke (caused by tiny clots in the brain). This, however, has never been shown to be a significant issue with pills. Yet even if this were true, a woman's flow when on the pill is generally so light that it's doubtful much iron is expelled through the monthly cycling. If this were a legitimate concern, we would have already detected it through the millions of women years of COC use.

Potential risk of cancer of the breast and the uterus needs to be determined, however. The original monthly COC contraceptive approach has been exhaustively studied, and anything new will have to compare favorably with its track record.

The Pill: Fast FAQs

Question: What's the difference between twenty-one-day pills, twenty-eight-day pills, and the other types of pills?

Answer: With the exception of Seasonale, most pills come packaged in twenty-one or twenty-eight-day prescriptions, both of which contain twenty-one active pills. The main difference is that the twenty-eight-day packs includes seven placebo pills, which contain *no* hormone. So the only real difference is that women using the twenty-one-day packs have to remember to start the next pack on the right day, while those using a twenty-eight-day pack never interrupt their habit of taking a daily pill. For low-dose pills to work reliably, patients *must* take them regularly, preferably at the same time of day.

Sometimes the placebo pills include a little iron to compensate for menstrual flow, but the amount of iron in these tiny pills probably has little impact.

Question: Can you continue taking the pill so that you skip your period? Is that safe? I just realized that my period is going to come when I am on vacation.

Answer: We certainly have ways of altering the onset of a woman's menstrual flow using the artificial hormones in pills. Consult with your physician, who knows your history, the type of pill you are taking, and how much shifting is reasonable. Doctors receive these sorts of requests regularly, so don't hesitate to ask. Do, however, hesitate to make the changes on your own or on the advice of a friend.

Question: I've been told that being on birth control pills would relieve some of my menstrual symptoms. So far I've had less pelvic pain and fewer twinges during the month and fewer bowel problems. But I just started my period and the flow seems to be as heavy as always, which is very heavy. Do you have to be on the pill for a while to see more improvement?

Answer: It takes time for the low-estrogen environment of the COCs to exert maximal effect in certain conditions, such as endometriosis (endometrial tissue in places outside the uterus, such as on the ovaries, pelvic organs, or bladder) and adenomyosis (endometrial tissue within the muscular part of the uterine wall).

Also, different pill concentrations are appropriate for certain diagnoses. Consult with your physician and keep good records of any changes in your symptoms. This will greatly aid in your doctor's ability to make a positive change in your medication dosage. Though not directly pertaining to contraception, the relief of heavy menstrual flow is another valuable and common application of COCs.

Question: How effective is the pill in preventing pregnancy?

Answer: Currently, COCs have a greater than 99 percent efficiency per 100 women years of usage. That is, if one hundred women used the pill for a year, one woman at most would get pregnant, assuming proper usage and no confounding variables. But people get sick, skip pills, take them late, and take other medications that reduce the pill's effectiveness, so confounding variables happen fairly often.

Question: How effective is the pill if I forget to take it once in a while?

Answer: A survey released by the American Medical Women's Association and Ortho-McNeil, a pharmaceutical company, showed that 59 percent of women do forget to take their birth control.[3] In a French study of more than 2,800 women, two-thirds of unplanned pregnancies occurred among women who described themselves as using contraception. Of these, 21 percent reported using birth control pills, with four out of five of this group saying they had missed one or more pills.[4] Anyone considering taking the pill *must* take it as prescribed.

Question: Are pills safe?

Answer: The right pill for the right woman has a good margin of safety, but each hormone carries risks. Every woman must consider factors such as age, medical history, history of past surgeries, smoking, alcohol use, and illicit drug use. Any of these factors may decrease the margin of safety or even make the pill unsuitable for a specific woman's use.[5]

Years ago the pill was less safe than it is today. The newer pills do not appear to have adverse effects on the cardiovascular system, as did earlier versions, and the newer pills offer a range of noncontraceptive health benefits.[6] For example, COCs seem to reduce the risk of ovarian and endometrial cancer. They also reduce the incidence of benign breast diseases, such as fibrocystic changes and benign cysts, though this has not been demonstrated to clearly reduce breast cancer risk. In addition, COCs considerably reduce the incidence of benign ovarian cysts. And by thickening the cervical mucus, COCs reduce the risk of pelvic inflammatory disease by about 50 percent. They have other health benefits as well.

Known risks appear to be dose dependent to some extent. The pill appears to cause an increase of blood clots in the veins, which disappears quickly when the COC is stopped. The COC also doubles the risk of hemorrhagic stroke, a risk related to smoking and hypertension. Much of this information, however, is based on studies involving older, high-dose COCs. Risks may well be lower with modern COCs, but we don't yet have enough information to know for certain.[7]

Question: If the wife is on the pill, can a couple have sex anytime?

Answer: Yes. If taken correctly, the pills provide protection throughout the month, including the week off or the placebo-pill week. Spontaneity is one of the most attractive features of COCs.

Question: During the time I'm on the pill, will my eggs that would otherwise ovulate be preserved, thus prolonging my fertility?

Answer: Research is under way that will tell us the exact effect of contraception on menopausal age, but to date we have nothing definite. So far there's no convincing evidence that pill use delays menopause. In fact, many researchers believe that while a woman is on the pill and even when she's pregnant, eggs continue to diminish in number. Others think eggs are indeed preserved during this time, but when ovulation resumes, the most sensitive eggs join those maturing. (For example, you might have twelve to fourteen follicles starting out instead of ten, though still only one would become dominant and ovulate.) Yet when it comes to fertility, the issue is not so much the *number* of eggs and whether you'll run out, but rather the *quality* of eggs. You only need one egg, but it must be of good quality, and that quality is affected by age.

Question: Can pill use lead to infertility due to the alteration of a woman's body chemistry?

Answer: It's unlikely that pill use leads to infertility. The pill suppresses ovulation. Women who ovulated regularly before going on the pill will generally resume ovulation within about a month after going off the pill. The pill doesn't cure irregular periods, however. Women who were irregular before going on the pill will probably be irregular after going off the pill. In other words, the pill simply sends the orchestra on vacation. If members didn't play well when they left, they probably won't have improved once they return. A woman whose ovulation fails to return within two months of going off the pill should consult her doctor.

Using the Pill: Risky Business?

For health reasons, some women must avoid taking COCs. These may include patients with the following:

- Kidney disease
- Liver problems
- History of blood clots
- Disease of the adrenal glands
- History of stroke
- History of coronary artery disease
- Breast cancer
- Cancer of the endometrium
- Abnormal vaginal bleeding, unless/until a definitive diagnosis is made
- Smokers, especially those over age thirty-five

Such a list tells us that taking COCs is serious business. Altering the body's hormonal rhythm must not to be undertaken lightly. It also suggests how foolish it is to take a friend's pills. Yet while these warnings are significant, they actually apply only to a narrow sampling of fertile women. Most young, healthy women can take COCs without significant risk, and doctors can usually find a suitable prescription for a woman desiring COCs.

In addition to the conditions listed above, women considering hormonal contraceptive approaches should know about their potential side effects. Some are minor and self-limited; others are more serious.

- Pill use can possibly increase the risk of problems with blood lipids (such as alterations in low-density lipoprotein and high-density lipoprotein ratios), which may be significant in heart disease.
- In rare cases, a liver tumor—generally benign—follows pill use.
- Many women note some degree of fluid retention and weight gain.
- Many women report emotional changes, mood swings, and depression.
- Unpredictable spotting, particularly in the first few cycles of use, is common, though most women tolerate it well.
- The pill's estrogen level may be lower than that to which the patient is accustomed. The result may be decreased vaginal lubrication and elasticity as well as vaginal dryness, making intercourse uncomfortable. Such patients may require lubricants for intercourse and a more gradual progression to full penetration.
- Some women develop headaches.
- Some contact-lens wearers have noted significant visual changes or dryness.
- Drug interactions with the pill are well known. Other medications may decrease the effectiveness of COCs. These include antibiotics, anticonvulsants (seizure medications), Saint-John's-wort, and perhaps Tylenol and vitamin C.
- The pill can cause lowered libido. In one woman's words, "When I'm on the pill, I don't care about sex at all. When I'm off the pill, I have a happy husband. We've been together fifteen years, and that has always been the case." Women have roughly one-tenth the circulating testosterone that men have, and the pill tends to decrease androgen (male hormone, which women make in small amounts) production from the ovary. Generally, lowered libido can be managed by changing the type of pill prescribed.

- Some patients have an altered sensitivity to smell.[8]
- Some women with a genetic predisposition for breast cancer who took COCs before age thirty or before 1975 may have an increased risk of breast cancer.[9]

When we consider all these factors, why would anyone want to take the pill? First is reliability. Second is convenience. Hormonal contraception can bring an element of spontaneity into the romantic relationship. Yet these benefits alone would not account for the widespread popularity of the pill and its use over the past decades. It has some other benefits too.

Proper pill use generally makes the menstrual flow lighter, less painful, and highly predictable. The pill's relatively fast reversibility adds to its attractiveness. That is, couples don't have to wait a long time after stopping it to try to have children.

Additionally, while some patients find the pill makes their PMS worse, others say it helps. Women with persistent ovarian cysts, endometriosis, painful periods, or heavy periods, may find the pill relieves their symptoms. COCs often work well in the treatment of a multitude of gynecological problems, even when contraception is not the primary goal.

Generally, if a woman misses one pill, she should take it as soon as she remembers or take two the following day. If she misses two days, it is recommended that she stop taking the pills, use alternate protection, wait for her menstrual flow to start, and then restart a new pack of pills. (She can save the leftover pills for days when she drops one on the floor.)

Progesterone-Only Pills (POPs)

As the name suggests, progesterone-only pills (POPs) contain no estrogen. Instead, they rely on small amounts of progesterone to block the pituitary function and prevent the LH surge that triggers ovulation. The continuous, low dose of progesterone also makes the cervical mucus less favorable than it would be in a regular ovulatory cycle.

Physicians often prescribe POPs for women who do not tolerate estrogen well because of side effects such as migraines. POPs are also sometimes recommended for nursing mothers whose babies have begun to sleep through the night.

Current studies suggest that progesterone-only pills have a considerably higher breakthrough-ovulation rate than combination methods do, thus making POPs potentially riskier in terms of possible pregnancy or an abortifacient action. The uterine lining of a patient on POPs will be thin, as no estrogen primes the lining for the embryo. At the time of ovulation, the ovary increases its own estrogen production, and progesterone would rise as well. Would this be sufficient to prevent the hostile endometrial environment that might lead to spontaneous miscarriage? No one can say with certainty. Because the "accidental" ovulation rate may be as much as ten times higher than with COCs, however, special consideration should be given to this issue before beginning POPs.

Most of the Christian physicians with whom I've spoken agree that patients ought to be informed of how each hormonal approach affects the body. POPs may prove to present a high enough level of risk for a developing embryo to warrant a statement against their use.

While the pill is highly effective in preventing pregnancy, there are some concerns about how it works. In addition to preventing fertilization, does the pill actually cause abortion? Both sides in the debate have been guilty of misinformation. In the next chapter, we'll try to further separate myth from fact.

LET'S TALK ABOUT IT

1. What had you heard about the pill before reading this? Was what you'd heard fairly accurate?
2. What, in your own circumstances, do you see as the most important pros and cons of pill use?
3. For her: Do you have any health conditions that would put you at risk if you took the pill?
4. For her: Do you need to have any tests done to determine if the pill is safe for you?

CHAPTER 8

DO BIRTH CONTROL PILLS CAUSE ABORTION?

I think deep down I did not want to think that for years I had already been doing something so awful by taking the pill.

I never knew this. Should I feel guilty?

We shouldn't lay guilt on people by talking about this.

We shouldn't tell people the pill might cause abortions because once they know, they'll be responsible for the information. The pill resulted in greatly expanded opportunities for women, who enjoy more education, better jobs and careers, and fuller lives around the world.

The pill has led to the disintegration of the nuclear family, promiscuity, teen sex, and a host of other societal ills. It ought to be banned.

In terms of the how the pill works, no egg is available and few sperm can get through the cervix to swim in the neighborhood—so no pregnancy. That's in an ideal situation. Yet as we discussed in the last chapter, confounding variables often arise. Does ovulation sometimes happen despite efforts to prevent it? Yes. This is known as breakthrough or escape ovulation. We know breakthrough ovulation happens, because women taking the pill as directed sometimes still get pregnant. Do we know how often breakthrough ovulation happens or if, when it does, it places the embryo at risk? No. Statistics taken from studies conducted in the past five years suggest that ovulation occurs between less than 1 percent and 5 percent of cycles in which no pills were missed.[1]

Should women therefore avoid taking the pill due to sanctity-of-life considerations? Researchers, practitioners, theologians, and patients debate this question vigorously.

> *I was on a low-dose pill when I learned in my embryology under-graduate class about the "third mechanism of action" of the pill [thinning the uterine lining], by an objective atheist professor. We have been practicing natural family planning ever since.*

The Effect of the Pill on the Lining of the Uterus

Check out most pro-life websites that are seeking answers for whether the pill causes abortion, and invariably you will find the annually released *Physicians Desk Reference* (PDR) mentioned. For years, the PDR has stated that one of the ways the pill works is by changing the endometrium, the uterine lining. Researchers of the day recognized that patients on oral contraceptive pills (OCPs) had lighter periods due to lower estrogen, and estrogen is responsible for endometrial growth. They used phrases such as "inhospitable" and "hostile" to describe the likely effects of birth control pills on the endometrium. At that time, researchers had no direct method of measuring or confirming the adverse endometrial effect during break-through ovulation. Now with our ability to test serum hormonal levels while observing the endometrial lining with ultrasonography, we should be able to determine what effect breakthrough ovulation has on the endometrium.

Still, what could this finding mean? Considering the known risk of breakthrough ovulation, it's possible that an egg might be released and be fertilized in the fallopian tube only to have the embryo arrive at the uterus to find an unfavorable endometrium. The hostile uterine environment could potentially be incompatible with human life, and the embryo would die.

This is significant when we consider the value of each individual human life from the moment of fertilization. By the time the human embryo travels down the fallopian tube and arrives at the uterus, it may consist of 150 to 200 cells in a ball-like structure called a blastocyst. If we have interfered with the blastocyst's efforts to implant in the uterus, we have a morally unacceptable situation. In the sequence of events described above, the pill would prevent implantation rather than prevent ovulation or fertilization, making the OCP an abortifacient (abortion-causing medication).

Although the progesterone in the pills thickens the cervical mucus, thus blocking the entry point for sperm, progesterone's effects on the endometrium do raise significant questions. The thinning of the uterine lining seen during a nonovulatory cycle of a woman using OCPs could make successful implantation less likely, all things being the same. The question that remains, however, is whether the increasing hormone levels needed for breakthrough ovulation would alter the lining sufficiently to permit successful implantation.

What If . . .

Let's suppose breakthrough ovulation occurs and a clever sperm has sneaked through hostile mucus and has fertilized an egg. Does that mean the developing embryo will find a hostile landing zone once it reaches the uterus? This is an important question. And Christian experts in many fields differ on the answer. They debate how thin the lining has to be to cause an increased risk of embryo death. An additional factor complicates the question: If enough messenger hormone gets through to cause ovulation in the first place, won't enough estrogen be produced by the maturing follicle and enough progesterone be released after ovulation to counteract the pill's negative effect on the uterine lining? If the pill has failed fundamentally in turning off the pituitary gland, as evidenced by ovulation, that means there had to have been some increased estrogen production. Would it be sufficient to thicken the uterine lining enough to make it safe for implantation?

At least a few days of increasing estrogen levels are necessary for the egg to mature before ovulation. This would certainly affect the endometrial lining and change the cervical mucus, possibly overriding the effect of the low-dose pills. The human egg cannot be released in ovulation without a surge of LH (luteinizing hormone); ovulation requires the LH surge. The presence of ovulation would mean that the pill failed to suppress this surge. But LH does something else too. It stimulates the launch site for the egg to produce progesterone. Is the amount of progesterone now produced enough to adequately "sweeten" the lining and make it favorable for implantation?

Once the egg has been fertilized, it normally takes five to seven days for it to continue its journey and implant in the uterus. During this time, estrogen and progesterone production have increased by virtue of the breakthrough ovulation. Wouldn't this counterbalance all the effects of the pill?

Difficult to Prove

Obtaining accurate information to answer these questions is a challenge. First, breakthrough ovulation is a relatively rare event. Although sonograms confirm that women on OCPs sometimes have developing follicle cysts, most researchers say this doesn't necessarily mean an egg is released. Consider these findings:

- A study of 130 women who started oral contraceptives later in the cycle than recommended had significantly more ovarian follicular development, but the postponement did not appear to increase actual ovulation rates.[2] (Development of follicles, seen via ultrasound, does not mean breakthrough ovulation is inevitable, as some have claimed.)
- One study of ninety-nine women tested the hypothesis that omitting the first three pills of the contraceptive cycle leads to ovulation. The subjects were randomly assigned to one of three treatments of combination oral contraceptives (COCs). None of the women experienced normal ovulation as evaluated by ultrasound and serum progesterone concentrations. Follicle growth up to preovulatory size was common in women missing the first one to three pills of the contraceptive cycle, yet normal ovulation still did not occur when pill omissions were limited to only three days.[3]

In addition, the high miscarriage rate in otherwise normal pregnancies complicates the data. Experts estimate that half or more of normal pregnancies end in the miscarriage of early implantation embryos—most of which are lost before the woman knows she is pregnant. (We have this information today thanks to blood tests that confirm pregnancy.) To prove that OCPs cause embryos to be aborted and then to estimate the actual risk involved would require confirming that the pregnancy-loss rate in women with breakthrough ovulation and conception exceeds the already high early miscarriage rate.

Hormone production after breakthrough ovulation may well be normal, overriding the effects of the pill, as is evidenced by babies born to pill users.

Is Any Amount of Risk Acceptable?

Some have concluded that the existence of even the remote possibility of the embryo encountering an unprepared lining makes using OCPs immoral. While we understand and respect this position, we also believe it's helpful in decision making to know the estimated degree of risk.

Perhaps it's helpful to note that since I started in medical school more than thirty years ago, microwaves, cell phones, computer monitors, and ultrasounds have all been charged with causing first-trimester abortions.

While some people may consider these ridiculous suggestions, there was good scientific theory behind each of them. Take ultrasound, for example. When it was first developed in the 1970s, the machines were enormous and the resolution poor, but we began to see life developing in the womb. Some researchers took the sound wave and, by adjusting frequency and focus and targeting human tissue cultures, were able to cause cellular damage. Obviously, this caused quite an uproar with justifiably concerned patients and qualified physicists on either side of the issue. Were we causing damage to human babies by aiming sound waves at them? Others suggested that ultrasound would cause damage to the babies' ears. So early recommendations were that ultrasounds should only be performed in high-risk situations in which the unknown risk was exceeded by the potential benefit. Now, decades later, we appreciate that those concerns were perhaps overstated. But with the advent of new technology, including 3-D/4-D ultrasound, pulse-wave Doppler studies, and color Doppler studies of babies in utero, we are utilizing new forms of energy on embryos from the earliest stages without clarity as to the risk. The medical community currently recommends that ultrasound be performed only when necessary. In the case of ultrasound, energy is focused directly at the embryo and developing baby. Hormonal contraception targets the supporting environment, which is less direct. Yet each raises unique questions of risk.

Despite these concerns, we continue to selectively use ultrasound because we have determined that the risks are quite small in comparison with the benefits. Some would argue that the risks with OCPs are no different. Protection of human life is a concern in both situations. While we do not ignore these concerns, there is no proof that either ultrasound or OCPs cause harm.

Some say that when it comes to OCPs, we need to err on the side of life. Yet even where precious human life is concerned, we make decisions based on the risk-benefit ratio. For example, certain viral infections can have a devastating or fatal effect on the human embryo. If we are to take *no* risk with a pregnancy, do we quarantine all pregnant women? No. We weigh the risks of exposure against the benefits of daily functioning. Auto accidents are probably riskier to human life than contraceptive pills, yet we still drive; the risk of being struck by lightning may pose greater risk, yet we travel on cloudy days; an allergic reaction to antibiotics might kill us, but we still take them. We are used to making decisions based on risk-benefit ratios.

What are the risks when it comes to OCPs? If we knew definitively, we'd have come to a comfortable consensus within the faith community. Yet that is not the case. In the absence of clear evidence, wisdom demands, then, that we consider available knowledge and respond prayerfully. Recognizing that the best pro-life scientists disagree, perhaps we can extend grace to those who evaluate the data and come to differing conclusions.

What Does the Current Research Tell Us?

What information is available to us now about pill use? Consider the following:

- One hundred women were randomly assigned to receive one of two oral contraceptives over a single treatment cycle. Breakthrough ovulation was observed in three subjects in one group. Only one of these escape ovulations was considered the result of treatment failure (the patient either forgot her pills or took medications that reversed the pills' effects). None of the patients in the other group ovulated. No statistically significant difference was found between treatment groups.[4]

- One hundred eighteen women participated in a study that measured the impact of two low-dose oral contraceptives on suppression of ovarian activity, cervical mucus changes, and endometrial readiness. In the random double-blind study involving women recruited from ten study centers in Germany, data failed to document ovulation in any treatment cycle.[5]

- Fifty-three women (in a total of 109 cycles) received one of two combination low-dose oral contraceptives. The ability of the pills' formulations to inhibit ovulation was compared by measuring hormone levels and ultrasound monitoring. The effects on three treated cycles were compared with the women's pre- and post-treatment cycles. No ovulations occurred in either group during therapy.[6]

- Twenty-four healthy female volunteers with normal ovulatory cycles, between twenty and thirty-four years of age, were studied to investigate breakthrough ovulation.[7] None occurred.

What We Need to Know

Putting all the studies together, we see that breakthrough, or escape, ovulation is a rare event. But how can we know if the pill is responsible for abortions? Research will need to support or destroy the hypothesis that OCPs cause a thinning effect on the uterine lining *even when breakthrough ovulation occurs*. That will mean following many women on pills and measuring uterine changes, watching the ovaries for signs of ovulation, and then documenting endometrial thickness changes in breakthrough-ovulation cycles. To date no one has done this.

It's important to add here that, as any ob-gyn—and any pathologist—knows, an embryo does not require a perfectly prepared endometrium to implant. We've seen pregnancies implant in the fallopian tubes, on the ovaries, on the intestines, and even on other intra-abdominal structures that have no endometrium. In addition, recent *microscopic* studies of the endometrium demonstrate that we cannot predict receptivity based on thinness or thickness the uterine lining, raising new questions about the significance of observed endometrial thinning in COC cycles.[8] Most obstetricians have delivered babies that were conceived while the mothers were taking OCPs. These babies have done fine, and the risk of miscarriage or congenital abnormalities was no greater than for babies in the population at large.

This is not to say that any pregnancy can implant anywhere, nor does it minimize concerns about a possible abortifacient effect of the pill. Such concerns are, in fact, significant. They are so significant that every couple considering using OCPs should keep up with the latest developments on this subject.

Putting It Together—for Now

In my opinion, the evidence is interesting but not convincing that Christians should avoid COCs. I still prescribe them, but I explain to patients what we do and don't know. For patients with certain medical conditions, such as endometriosis, recurrent ovarian cysts, and abnormally heavy periods, the benefits of COC use are significant. Others should prayerfully consider alternatives to the pill and consult with their physicians to find the best methods of contraception to fit their needs. Based on the current research, I'm inclined to avoid the progesterone-only pill (POP) purely on a statistical basis and not based on any evidence that POPs have an abortifacient effect. My opinion is based on the fact that POPs have a considerably higher breakthrough-ovulation rate than COCs.

When it comes to contraception, like anything else, we have a responsibility to be informed, prayerful, and open to God's direction if his plans differ from ours, as they sometimes do. Those who choose to use the pill need to keep up with any new information that might either reveal new concerns or lay to rest current fears.

Most people have approached this as a "do or don't" subject: either take the pills or avoid them altogether. Yet there may be an "in between" option: a woman can take the pills but be vigilant about looking for signs of breakthrough ovulation. If such signs are present, she can use alternate protection or abstain from intercourse during her fertile days. For example, when a woman misses two or three pills in a row during a month, the medical recommendation is to use alternate protection. You can't trust the pill to work if you don't take it the way it's prescribed. The patient might have mid-cycle awareness of symptoms such as back pain, increasing vaginal discharge, and the abdominal sensations sometimes associated with impending ovulation. Additionally, she might include midcycle monitoring of salivary ferning patterns or even of urinary LH surges to better anticipate the rare breakthrough-ovulatory event. When such signs are observed, additional steps could be taken to avoid a potential ethical dilemma for those who value life. Such practices have not yet been researched, but they might be worth considering.

FAQs about Ethical Issues

Question: If I take the pill faithfully and make sure I don't take medications that can decrease its efficiency, can I be 100 percent sure that it will never cause an abortion?

Answer: No. Someone expecting a contraceptive method to have *zero possibility* of being an abortifacient should avoid the pill. But that doesn't mean it *is* an abortifacient or that it has ever, by itself, caused an abortion. While we value life at the one-cell stage, we must be fair and honest with the data. And at the moment, the findings are still unclear.

Question: When I take the pill, I don't intend to cause abortion. Doesn't intent matter?

Answer: Yes, from an ethical point of view, intent is important. The thousands of Christians now taking OCPs do not intend to cause miscarriage. In fact, they intend to prevent pregnancy. As we watch the medical research, however, our intent doesn't hold more weight than the evidence. While I may not intend to back my car over my neighbor, I should still look behind the car before throwing it in reverse and stomping on the gas.

Question: What do you think I should do? Take the pill or not?

Answer: Stay informed about the medical risks as they are currently understood. Be willing to learn as new data is revealed. Then prayerfully decide after consultation with your physician if you can use the pill before the question is more fully resolved. If you feel led to use this hormonal approach to contraception, make sure you use the pills as prescribed and always ask your physician about drug interactions if you receive a prescription for another medication. We know that taking OCPs regularly and avoiding interaction with some other medications will diminish the risk of breakthrough ovulation.

If you choose not to take the pill for reasons of conscience, be gentle with others who make choices differing from yours. And continue to educate yourself. If your doctor won't talk to you about it, find another physician. It's important to base medical decisions on solid information, not conjecture.

Question: How can I get past the fear I have that while I was taking the progesterone-only pill, I might have caused the abortions of my children?

Answer: Such concerns are matters of conscience, not necessarily matters of science. And matters of conscience are best handled with humility before the Lord, confessing decisions you made based on the available data and expressing concern for life's preciousness.

Question: If some day the research does prove that the pill causes abortion, wouldn't I look back with regret?

Answer: With the use of any medical intervention, whether diagnostic ultrasound or altering the hormonal environment, questions often remain about its effects. One does not have to have ultrasounds or use oral contraception, but there are benefits in certain cases that may outweigh the potential risks. Hopefully further research will answer some of the remaining questions.

As those who look to the Bible as our ultimate authority, we are used to having absolute answers on many topics. Thus, we can feel great discomfort with issues for which the answers are unclear. Solid Christian experts stand on both sides of this issue. Some say we should avoid the pill at all costs because it might cause abortion. Others remain unconvinced. Neither side knows for sure.

In my own practice, I delivered some babies that were conceived while their mothers were taking the pill. So I know from personal experience that if there is an abortive effect of the pill, it certainly cannot be so 100 percent of the time. Still, the answer at this writing is unclear. If you need absolutes, stay away from the pill but stay informed and consult your own physician. For now, taking COCs appears to be an ethical option, but we still face some unknowns and await further research.

The Christian Medical and Dental Associations, an organization of thousands of Christian doctors and dentists, has drafted a position statement about the possible postfertilization effects of hormonal birth control. For their complete statement on this matter, see appendix 2.

LET'S TALK ABOUT IT

1. Where does your physician stand on the subject of the ethics of the pill?
2. Is your physician willing to keep you updated on the latest research associated with taking the pill?
3. Are you willing to take an active role in staying informed about the pill as further research is done?
4. How much, if any, risk do you feel is acceptable?
5. For her: If you decide to use the pill, are you willing to also monitor the bodily signals that you might be ovulating?
6. For her: If you were to take the pill, for what duration would you feel comfortable taking it?

CHAPTER 9

OTHER HORMONE
THERAPY OPTIONS

I don't even know why I'm crying.

I'm spotting half the time. What a nuisance. I never know when it'll start or stop. To get together with my husband on Valentine's Day, I had to use a diaphragm, not for birth control but to keep the constant spotting from ruining our plans.

One day I love my husband, and the next day I want to yell at him.

Sometimes I just don't understand myself, so how can I expect him to understand me?

Women and their hormones are complex, often frustratingly so. Yet the complex design of a woman's reproductive system is not intended to make life difficult. Rather, it's part of the divine plan.

Scientists have carefully observed the beautiful delicacy of the female reproductive system and its hormones, and these researchers have found ways to harness that knowledge to give women more control of their lives. The chapter about combination oral contraceptives (COCs) focused on how the primary function of COCs is to give the ovaries a vacation, suppressing ovulation. In addition, the cervical mucus remains thick, making it tough for even the most tenacious of sperm to get through. And finally, the uterus is kept from developing its sweet, cushy lining; instead, it remains thin and unfavorable for implantation.

Other combination hormonal approaches—injections, implants, and vaginal rings—have approximately the same effect on the body, but they have the advantage of being less vulnerable to operator error.

What would the ideal hormonal contraceptive be like? First, it would be highly reliable. Second, it would be quickly reversible. That is, a couple desiring to conceive will want to be able to start trying within a month or two after stopping contraception. Third, to outdo the pill in terms of benefits, the ideal contraception would have no side effects such as spotting, nausea, and weight gain. An added plus would be to have a light but present, thus reassuring, menstrual flow. Certainly COCs fit the first qualification, as they *reportedly* have a greater than 99 percent effectiveness rate, assuming no confounding variables.

If a contraceptive approach with more than 99 percent effectiveness is available, why are so many pregnancies unplanned? Operator error is clearly a confounding factor, as in "Confound it! I forgot to take my pill" or "I forgot to *start* taking my pills." All of the hormonal contraceptive methods discussed so far require consistent use, something which proves challenging for many patients. For many women, then, perhaps the best approach to hormonal contraception isn't a daily pill after all.

The Lunelle Injection

After taking the pill for eight years, I switched. I like Lunelle because it's convenient, and I don't have to worry about forgetting a pill. I especially like the grace period of a few days that Lunelle allows before I have to receive my next injection.

No pills to remember, no upset stomach. For me it's contraceptive autopilot. I just make my next month's appointment when I get my shot, and the nurse calls to remind me the day before I'm due back. So far it's been foolproof.

The Lunelle injection is a combination of estrogen and a progesterone derivative (a progestin, which is a synthetic hormone with activity similar to natural progesterone). Lunelle is given in a single, monthly injection every twenty-eight to thirty (never more than thirty-three) days, in the arm, thigh, or buttock.

Given during one of the first five days of the menstrual cycle, Lunelle provides effective contraception. Lunelle is reportedly 99.8 percent effective in prevention of pregnancy when used correctly.[1] Among its advantages are unimpeded sex and having no responsibility to remember contraception on a daily basis. There are no patches or pills to buy or keep track of, and Lunelle costs about the same as birth control pills.

The injected hormones are absorbed directly into the bloodstream from the muscle at the injection site, bypassing the stomach. Because of how it's absorbed, Lunelle causes fewer problems with the liver and other medications interacting with hormones than do oral contraceptives. Another benefit that early trials suggest is a rapid return to fertility once injections are stopped.

The downside of Lunelle is that it requires a monthly visit to the health-care team for reinjection and, of course, the discomfort of the injections themselves. Weight gain is also a possible side effect, with women reporting an average gain of about four pounds in the first year.[2]

The Ortho Evra Contraceptive Patch

I've been on lots of different pills. A few made me puke; a few made me crazy. I'm currently on the patch, which is a once-weekly thing. I like it better than pills because I have to remember to use it only once a week. It's unobtrusive, costs the same as pills through my insurance, and I've had none of the irritability and nausea that the pills caused me.

The patch is ideal for me. No pills to take, and it stays on through aerobics class. Like they say, I took contraception off my mind and put it on my body.

The manufacturer says this is a great, concealable method of contraception. But it's not so concealable to a big segment of the population—those of us whose skin is much darker than the patch.

While the contraceptive patch is still an imperfect contraceptive, in its design it's getting closer to the ideal. About the size of a matchbook, the Ortho Evra contraceptive patch—approved in both the

United States and Canada—is as thin as a piece of tape, is water-proof, and won't fall off.

The patch currently comes in one color: beige. Manufacturers are working on a clear patch to appeal to a more ethnically diverse audience. They're also investigating the possibility of flowery decals that can be worn over patches, so perhaps one day patients will wear them conspicuously as body art. For now, a patient places her patch on the skin in a discreet place, such as the abdomen, buttocks, or chest (but not on a breast). She changes the patch weekly for three weeks and then goes without it for one week, allowing for menstrual flow.

The patch delivers the same types of hormones as those used in COCs, so it has similar risks. Because the patch is relatively new, its long-range safety has yet to be established. The Ortho Evra patches deliver hormones more effectively than the first-generation patches, however. Hormones pass from the patch through the skin and into the bloodstream, and patients are less likely to forget to change the patch than they are to forget to take a pill.[3] The cost currently runs between twenty-five and forty dollars per month.[4]

A side effect unique to the patch is sensitivity to the adhesive, which is why the manufacturer recommends moving the site of application with each patch change. Breast tenderness seems to be a common side effect as well, but that tends to diminish within three months. As with any hormonal approach, some unpredictable spotting may occur as the body adapts to the external hormone treatment.

The patch has been studied with active women to see if it is likely to come off or be rendered ineffective when exercising or participating in water activities. It appears to adhere well and to maintain a steady level of hormone.[5]

The patch is well tolerated and easy to use, since it's applied once a week for three weeks. Yet remembering to apply a new patch on the proper day can be an issue, as is true with any external hormonal application.

American Family Physician magazine reports that the Ortho Evra patch is about 97 percent effective in preventing pregancy.

The NuvaRing

I love the NuvaRing—really love it. It looks like a clear rubber bracelet. Once a month, you fold it up and insert it in the vagina for three weeks. Then you remove it, discard it, take a week off, and start afresh. My period is completely regular, and I've never had a problem.

Occasionally I use the NuvaRing for a month of birth control. But I try to avoid having something artificial inside me.

I like the NuvaRing. It isn't a barrier method, but it's closer to the heart of things, so to speak.

Another "once a month and then forget about it" method of contraception is the NuvaRing. It's a soft, flexible vaginal ring that is about two inches in diameter. It contains the same hormones commonly found in COCs.

A patient using the NuvaRing flattens it as she would a rubber band, then inserts it into her vagina as she would a tampon. Ideally, she does so on day one of her menstrual cycle, but it can be inserted up to day five.[6] She leaves it in the vagina for twenty-one days and then removes it. After a seven-day menstrual week, she inserts a new NuvaRing. The ring does not have to be perfectly placed to work. Most wives can't feel the NuvaRing once it's inserted, nor can their husbands. And typically, normal periods return quickly after stopping use.

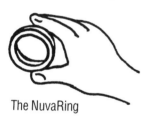

The NuvaRing

Unlike with COCs, the hormones released by a NuvaRing bypass the stomach. Instead, they penetrate directly through the vaginal wall, providing slow, steady delivery of the hormones. Because of this, the NuvaRing contains the least hormone of all the combination approaches and has an effectiveness rating that's comparable to, if not slightly higher than, COCs. The decreased amount of hormone means it also has fewer side effects.

The effectiveness of all hormone combination approaches may be lessened if a woman is overweight. If a patient's weight exceeds one hundred fifty pounds, she should consult her doctor about the best approach for her.

The contraceptive patch, shot, and ring have the advantages of a more predictable absorption rate and the maintenance of much steadier blood hormone levels than with pills. Pills are swallowed, absorbed by the stomach, and pass through the liver to the bloodstream, causing a rise and fall in hormone levels. During the hours following ingestion, hormone levels fall again until the next pill is taken. This rise and fall of hormone levels makes breakthrough ovulation and pituitary activation slightly more likely, increasing the chances that conception could occur. For the conscientious patient concerned with undesired ovulation, these approaches would appear to ensure a patient's steadier hormonal environment. Long-term follow-up studies are needed to demonstrate whether breakthrough ovulation actually occurs with these methods.

The Morning-After Pill, or "Emergency Contraception"

The morning-after pill is a bad idea. It acts to prevent a pregnancy by aborting a child.

I used the morning-after pill twenty years ago before knowing how it worked to cause an early abortion in some cases. I would not use it again now that I know the truth. I was angry to find out years later that I had not been given all the information needed to make an informed choice. I'm okay now, but I used to cry about it a lot.

Say "contraception," and you may evoke strong emotion. Say "morning-after pill," and the responses may blow your hair back and part it down the middle. Such forceful responses are due to ethical concerns surrounding this contraceptive approach.

The so-called morning-after pill, also known as "emergency contraception," can be taken in two different approaches. The first option is not one tablet, but a series of combination oral contraceptives taken to initially spike a woman's estrogen and progesterone. Then the patient abruptly stops taking any pills, causing hormone levels to plummet.

The second option is a progesterone-only pill (0.75 mg of levonorgesterel) taken as soon as possible (within seventy-two hours of unprotected intercourse) and the second tablet twelve hours later. This approach is designed to give a fairly high dose of progesterone and then withdraw it, thus disrupting the endometrial lining so it will slough off as an artificially induced period. This process significantly decreases the likelihood of embryo implantation.

Medical Considerations

Before ovulation. If a woman uses either of the morning-after pill approaches before ovulation has occurred, the best evidence suggests that the medication prevents ovulation. If she has access either to ultrasound imaging or to blood tests that measure natural hormone levels, it may be possible to establish that ovulation has not yet occurred. If so, the morning-after pill might be an ethical option for preventing ovulation. But getting access to a transvaginal ultrasound machine on short notice—crucial in decision making—may be difficult.

After ovulation. A huge ethical problem arises with the morning-after pill if it is taken after ovulation has occurred, making it likely that fertilization is about to occur or *has* occurred. In such cases, the medication works to prevent a live embryo from implanting in the uterus. Instead, the embryo will die without the patient ever knowing for sure whether she was pregnant. This is *ethically unacceptable* from the standpoint of the sanctity of human life.[7]

Taking the morning-after pill before ovulation (as verified by ultrasound) differs significantly from using it in a day-to-day situation to abort a pregnancy resulting from unplanned, unprotected sexual activity.

In terms of risks and benefits, the same medical concerns apply as with COCs, such as blood clotting complications, heart attack, and stroke. In fact, such concerns are magnified, as the morning-after pill contains the same hormones as do COCs and POPs (progesterone-only pills) but is taken in the form of a high-dose pill in multiple doses (several pills are taken at one time).

I used the morning-after pill. I vomited twelve times in three hours. I had to be taken from work to the hospital in an ambulance. Then I spent six hours in the emergency room with an IV and oxygen.

A physician who is a member of the Christian Medical Association put it this way: "I'm concerned that some individuals may use [the morning-after pill] as their primary method of birth control, taking frequent doses of the medication. We have ample evidence that low-dose contraceptives taken in the usual manner for contraception are quite safe. But to my knowledge no one has demonstrated that relatively high doses (such as those present in the morning-after pill) taken frequently are safe. [Such] use of the medication could compound the incidence of otherwise relatively rare complications."

Obviously, the morning-after pill is not a contraceptive method to be used with any sort of regularity, even if a patient uses it before ovulation. We call it "emergency contraception" for a reason.

Progesterone-Only Approaches

Depo-Provera

With Depo-Provera, I think about contraception only four times a year. No remembering a pill every day, no monthly pharmacy run, no packing something for nights away from home, no worrying after missing a pill—because there's no pill to miss. Oh, and there's no patch peeking out from under my bikini at the beach. Birth control doesn't get much better than this.

Those who don't mind needles actually have several options available. The progesterone shot, called Depo-Provera, is given roughly every three months. Depo-Provera is highly effective in preventing conception by keeping the ovaries in a state of rest, preventing egg release. And no egg means sperm have nothing to fertilize, so pregnancy can't happen. Although one of the ways Depo-Provera works is by altering the uterine lining, the dose of progesterone is apparently high enough to suppress ovulation, so fertilization rarely takes place.

Depo-Provera is used extensively in more than ninety countries, due primarily to its relatively low cost. In fact, it made headlines during the apartheid era in South Africa when it was reported that black women were being given the drug immediately after giving birth without their knowledge or consent. It was banned in Zimbabwe in the 1980s because of fears about its side effects but is now available in South African clinics, along with a range of other contraceptive options.[8]

A disadvantage of Depo-Provera is that once an injection is given, there's no reversing its effects. (It's impossible to be "uninjected.") And return of ovulation is extremely unpredictable. Some women who menstruated regularly before getting the shots have failed to ovulate for up to a year after their last shot.

As with other forms of hormonal birth control, many women using Depo-Provera experience side effects. The most common are irregular periods or spotting. Some patients stop having periods altogether after a few months on the medication, and some may experience a slight weight gain. Depo-Provera has also been associated with a decrease in bone density.[9]

Progesterone Implants (Norplant, Implanon, Jadelle)

Imagine going to the doctor's office once and then forgetting about contraception for the next five years. Sounds good until you find you have breakthrough bleeding most days of the year. Or you gain fifty pounds. Or you start growing hair in unusual places. Or you frequently have to say, "Honey, I have a headache," because of all your migraines. That's what happened to a number of women on Norplant.

Norplant was a contraceptive delivery system that put progesterone in six plastic rods the size of matchsticks, which were placed just under the skin in the upper arm. Because of its low-dose progesterone-only approach, it also had a higher potential for breakthrough ovulation than do combination methods. Norplant was taken off the U.S. market in 2002.

In its place, along came Implanon, a single-rod implant placed under the arm. Implanon, which is not yet marketed in the United States at the time of this writing, provides nearly foolproof contraceptive protection for up to three years. Insertion requires a simple procedure performed by a physician, and the implant can be removed at any time. After removal, fertility is rapidly restored to preimplant status. Like other progesterone-only contraceptives, Implanon works by suppressing ovulation. It is associated with irregular menstrual bleeding and sometimes the complete absence of monthly bleeding.

Similar to Implanon is Jadelle, which uses two rods. For women who do not tolerate estrogen well, Implanon and Jadelle—which should be on the market soon—are worth considering. They contain the lower-dose progesterone, however, with the accompanying long-term thinning of the lining of the uterus. Little data is available to indicate what might happen if breakthrough ovulation were to occur on these levels of progesterone.

The Intrauterine Device (IUD)

I had always thought IUDs were dangerous. I was skeptical, but decided to give it a try. I've never looked back.

I liked the idea of using an IUD, but I was concerned that it worked as an abortion agent rather than actually preventing fertilization.

The IUD has a rich and storied history, starting with the ancient sages who discovered that a peach pit, a stone, or any other foreign object placed in a camel's uterus prevented it from getting pregnant. Thus began the technique of inserting something into the uterus to prevent pregnancy. Modern researchers developed new technologies based on the same concept, and today we have plastic devices of various shapes that serve the same function.

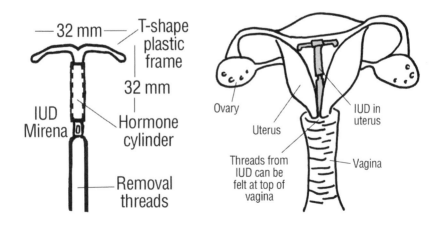

The IUD is neither a barrier method nor a hormonal approach, though some IUDs have a little bit of the hormone progesterone, such as in the IUD Mirena. Others contain copper, an element that statistics suggest improves IUD effectiveness, perhaps by creating a sterile, inflammatory response that kills sperm or prevents the embryo from implanting. Hormone-containing IUDs decrease menstrual cramping and bleeding.

Some older models of the IUD caused perforation and infection, so the method generally fell into disuse in this country because of the legal risk to manufacturers and physicians. It is currently experiencing a slight resurgence in popularity, however, because manufacturers have developed a smaller model for women who have never been pregnant.

Many women consider the IUD an ideal solution to family planning. Once in place, the IUD can be left in the uterus for years, and the method is quite effective in accomplishing its intended goal.

A competent physician or nurse practitioner inserts the IUD, so the cost involves the device itself and the doctor's visit, which may be two hundred dollars or more. Removal requires a return visit.

The advantages—besides fostering spontaneity—include round-the-clock protection without forethought. The IUD is highly effective, ranging from roughly 92 percent for nonhormonal IUDs to 98 percent for those that include hormones. Fertility returns for most women within one cycle after removal. Yet because the IUD can be left in for several years, the time frame for health problems and litigation potential increases.

Other problems with IUDs include increased menstrual bleeding and cramping for some women, along with increased risk of uterine infection, which can lead to infertility and even sterility. In addition, the device occasionally passes out of the uterus undetected, leaving the woman unprotected.

The IUD: How Ethical Is It?

There's another possible disadvantage to the IUD: how it works. While debate is ongoing, most researchers and physicians believe the IUD works not only by preventing fertilization but also by keeping

American Family Physician magazine summarizes the pros and cons of the IUD as follows:

IUD Advantages

1. Ease of compliance (once in, it's in; it works until you take it out)
2. Highly effective—as effective as female sterilization
3. Ten-year duration with ParaGard brand; five years with Mirena
4. Reduced menstrual bleeding with Mirena

IUD Disadvantages

1. High initial cost
2. Increased risk of PID (pelvic inflammatory disease)
3. Requires skilled insertion and removal by physician
4. Risk of uterine perforation (greatest at time of insertion)
5. Pain and bleeding increase leads to 5 to 15 percent discontinuing the technique
6. If pregnancy occurs, it's often complicated by presence of IUD
7. Spontaneous expulsion, especially in first few months
8. No protection against STIs*

*"The Intrauterine Device (IUD)," *American Family Physician*, December 1998, http://www.findarticles.com/cf_dls/m3225/ 9_58/53476366/p1/ article.jhtml (accessed March 27, 2004).

the human embryo from implanting in the uterus. If this is the case, the IUD is an abortifacient and raises significant ethical objections.

Historically, the best information available from research and experience suggests that the IUD does work as an abortifacient, with the possible exception of Mirena, which contains the same progesterone as Norplant did, which potentially could affect ovulation.[10] Thus, pregnancy begins normally in the fallopian tube, but the foreign object in the uterus keeps the embryo from implanting and developing. If this is the case, using an IUD is inconsistent with respecting the sanctity of life. Some doctors even insert IUDs after a woman has had intercourse, as a morning-after approach to contraception.

A few scattered researchers, however, argue that the IUD works not by preventing implantation but as a spermicidal agent, preventing the sperm (by an intrauterine inflammatory reaction) from ever reaching the egg. Currently available research remains unconvincing, and further studies with larger trial groups are required before we will have a definitive answer. Yet it's encouraging to note that a small group of laparoscopic studies has failed to detect viable sperm in the fallopian tubes of women with IUDs in place. This may suggest that IUDs work through a direct effect on the sperm rather than solely through creating a hostile intrauterine environment. If it can be conclusively demonstrated that IUDs do not work by preventing implantation of the growing embryo, the ethical obstacle will be eliminated. This would make the IUD a suitable contraceptive method for some couples. Key candidates would be couples who believe their family size is complete but who feel uncomfortable with permanent sterilization.

We need to consider new research as it unfolds, while making well-informed decisions based on the best information available now. Additionally, we must be gracious to those who use this technique, recognizing that many physicians don't clearly explain the potential mechanism of action to their patients. I've had couples become aware of the potential abortifacient action after many years of IUD use. While the evidence of an abortifacient action isn't absolute, couples should be aware of the possibility and make decisions based on the data.

A variety of options exist for couples desiring to prevent pregnancy. Each option has its own degree of effectiveness, convenience, privacy, reversibility, frequency of use, reliance on human memory, and ethical considerations. The chart on the following page provides an at-a-glance summary of some of the contraceptive methods we've discussed.

The altering of hormonal functions represents a major change in body chemistry. Thus, as part of the decision-making process, couples

	Monthly injection	Implant	IUD	Ring	The Pill	Barrier Methods	Patch
Effective	99.8%	99.8%	92-98%	97%	99+%*	88-97%*	97%
Doctor visits	Monthly	Insert/ remove	Insert/ remove	Rx	Semi-annually	Fitting for cap and diaphragm	Rx
Reversible	Readily	Surgical removal	Dr. visit	Readily	Yes	Yes	Readily
Frequency	1 month	Years	5 years	Monthly	Daily	As needed	Monthly
Memory required	No	No	No	Yes	Yes	Yes	Yes
Discreet	Yes	Somewhat	Yes	Mostly	Yes	No	Somewhat
Abort-ifacient?	No	Probably not	Question-able	No	Question-able	No	No

*Assuming proper usage

should include serious prayer and discussion with the prescribing physician. Taking man-made hormones to alter the menstrual cycle has medical, psychological, and even spiritual ramifications. While current evidence does suggest that hormonal contraceptive methods are safe for many women, they're not for everyone. Those who feel their families are complete but who are uncomfortable with, or not yet ready for, surgical sterilization often use the IUD or some of the longer-acting methods. Yet for some couples, the day will come when the more permanent options of tubal ligation and vasectomy look more appealing. We'll consider those options in the next chapter.

LET'S TALK ABOUT IT

1. How comfortable are you with the thought of using contraceptive methods that alter hormones?
2. How comfortable is your spouse with using hormonal contraceptives?
3. Of the methods presented here, which is the most attractive to you? Which is the least attractive? Why?
4. If you are comfortable using one of these methods, would you put a limit on how long you'd use it?

CHAPTER 10

UNDER THE KNIFE

PROCEDURES FOR HER

We're planning to minister in a third-world country. We already have three kids, and we'd like to keep our family size what it is now. I shudder at the thought of delivering a child in a place where good health care is so scarce.

I just had another miscarriage. Could I survive if it happened again? I don't know. Maybe I should just get my tubes tied and be done with it.

My doctor told me that having more kids would endanger my health. Besides, we want to homeschool our kids, and another pregnancy—or two or three—would make that impossible.

"Permanent" Sterilization

Angela Clark was thirty-five when she had her tubes tied, the grand finale in a long sequence of contraceptive disappointments. During the first two years of her marriage, she took the pill, but that killed her sexual desire. She and her husband switched to condoms, but, as Angela says, "he complained that he couldn't feel anything." Concerned about the effect of long-term hormonal therapy on her body and wanting to prevent the unintentional abortions she believed the IUD caused, Angela tried the diaphragm. "Ugh," she says, wrinkling her nose as she recalls how she would have to stop in the middle of a spontaneous romantic encounter to fill the cup with spermicide. "The diaphragm rated right up there with abstinence for me."

Later, wanting to avoid what she describes as "the mess," she switched to the Today Sponge, but then the FDA removed it from the market. "All that kind of puts a damper on your sex life."

For a growing number of women like Angela, challenges in the bedroom find their solution in the operating room. The latest information available from the National Center for Health Statistics tells us that female sterilization is the number one contraceptive choice among women in the United States.[1] More than 180 million women worldwide have had "a tubal," including an estimated seven hundred thousand Americans a year.[2]

A little over ten years ago, the method of choice was the pill, but not anymore. A breakdown of the statistics tells us that in 1995 (the latest data available), 24 percent of married women reported having had tubal ligations, and another 7 percent reported having had hysterectomies. Forty-one percent of married women between the ages of fifteen and forty-four reported that either they or their husbands had undergone a sterilizing operation. For baby boomers at the latter end of the reproductive years—between ages forty and forty-four—nearly 70 percent relied on either male or female sterilization. The survey revealed another interesting piece of information: an increasing number of women choose sterilization after only one or two births, compared with three or four births in years past. And women are three times more likely than men to have such a procedure.

The most common reason women choose tubal ligation (or tubal sterilization, or to "have their tubes tied") is simply that they have one or more children and feel their family is complete. Tubal ligation is an operation in which a surgeon blocks the fallopian tubes, which may actually be tied, cut, cauterized with electricity, or pinched closed with plastic clips or rubber bands. The individual doctor's preference and circumstances dictate the procedure of choice. Whatever means is used, the result is that the blocked tubes prevent egg and sperm from meeting. This procedure is often done through a laparoscope, a small telescope inserted into an incision in the abdominal wall that allows the doctor to view the internal organs. The cost of the operation runs between one and three thousand dollars.

Removing the ovaries (oophorectomy) or removing the uterus (hysterectomy) will also cause sterility, but such procedures carry more risk and side effects. Besides, doctors can access the tubes with relative ease. In fact, some techniques allow tubal interruption or blocking to be done as an outpatient operation.

In the United States, more than 90 percent of surgical sterilizations take place in hospitals or surgical centers using general anesthesia. There's a four- to five-hour recovery time, and the employed woman will miss three or four days of work.

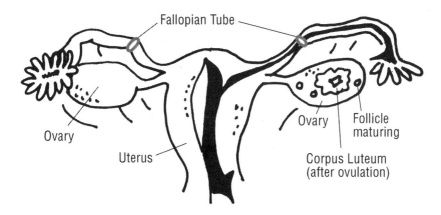

Choosing Sterilization: A Variety of Reasons

Factors other than frustration with various contraceptives drive the decision to opt for sterilization. Reasons vary as much as the people who pursue sterilization surgery.

- Jake and Lucy feel satisfied with their family size of four children. Lucy is thirty-seven and Jake is forty. Though female sterilization is more invasive and expensive than vasectomy, Jake says he can't get past associating vasectomy with castration. So Lucy is having the surgery.
- Jerry and Cindy are thirty-four and thirty-five respectively. Cindy had a difficult first pregnancy due to high blood pressure. Shortly after that, she learned she was pregnant again.

The doctor advised them that having a third child would be too risky for Cindy's health. The couple felt they would be content with two children. During the second pregnancy, they discussed the best options and chose for Cindy to have her tubes tied while she was still anesthetized from the epidural following birth. But when the doctor delivered their baby, the infant was having difficulty breathing. Together they all decided it would be best for Cindy to wait six weeks before doing anything permanent.

"A request for permanent sterilization is not a demand," the doctor explained later. "If something happens that confounds the decision-making process, flexibility is important."

The child improved so much that at the six-week checkup, Cindy went ahead with the surgery. "It was inconvenient to have to come back later," she said. "But I appreciated being able to make a decision apart from the stress and worry of a tough delivery."

- Tim and Debra are in their midthirties. Debra says, "We have three kids, and our family size feels right for us. Why spend the next decade hassling with contraception?"

When "Permanent" Isn't Permanent

Clearly, a variety of reasons motivate people to consider so-called permanent sterilization—vasectomy for him, tubal ligation for her. Before outlining the options, we must clarify that we say "so-called" because there's some flexibility on the "permanent" part.

In other words, sometimes patients have reversals. We also acknowledge the sovereignty of God, who is able to work around vasectomies and tubal ligations.

I'm thirty-seven, and I had a tubal ligation four years ago when I had a C-section with my last daughter. I have a twelve-year-old and a four-year-old. I took a home pregnancy test two days ago, and it came back positive. I'm five weeks pregnant. I guess the Lord decided we needed that boy after all.

Permanent procedures are never *easily* reversible in the same way that going off the pill or the patch can easily restore fertility. So while it's possible to surgically reverse vasectomies and tubal ligations in some instances (and God can certainly answer prayers for the impossible), patients should still avoid such procedures unless they're certain they desire no more children. Husbands and wives must weigh carefully the unlikely possibilities of death, divorce, and other catastrophes. They must also prayerfully consider whether they believe a decision to be surgically sterilized would honor God.

Postpartum Tubal

The most commonly done sterilization procedure is the postpartum tubal ligation (to "ligate" means to tie) done immediately following childbirth while the patient is still under the effects of the epidural or general anesthesia, as with a C-section. A laparoscope is not used in these cases because the increased uterine size brings the tubes near the umbilicus, making the scope unnecessary and even dangerous.

When performing a postpartum tubal, the surgeon makes a small incision in the crease of the lower half of the navel. This incision is continued, layer by layer, into the abdominal cavity. Then, through an opening just large enough to insert one finger, the uterus is manipulated and turned so that the appropriate tube is visible or palpable. The tube is grasped with an instrument and identified by following it to the fingerlike (fimbriated) end (see figure). A loop of the tube is tied off, and the intervening segment of each is cut out. After completing this process for each tube, the surgeon then sews the incision,

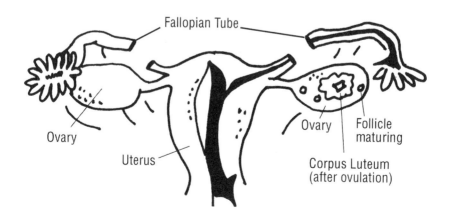

Fallopian Tube

Ovary

Ovary

Follicle maturing

Uterus

Corpus Luteum (after ovulation)

covers it with a Band-Aid, and sends specimens from the cut segments to pathology. This is to confirm that a tubal ligation has indeed been performed. If a tube grows back together, the pathology report helps to prove that the procedure was done correctly.

Couples should take special care when making the decision for a postpartum tubal. A decision made in the heat of the moment can be so emotional that it fails to reflect long-term wishes, particularly if the pregnancy was complicated or if the labor and delivery were stressful.

Mini-Laparotomy

A physician doing a mini-laparotomy, called a "mini-lap," performs the procedure apart from delivery. A mini-lap is a small operation done without the use of a laparoscope. Rather than making an incision at the navel, the surgeon makes an incision at the pubic hairline and extends the incision down into the abdominal cavity. Once the tubes are located manually, they're elevated up through the incision, identified, and tied and cut.

A mini-laparotomy requires anesthesia, usually general anesthesia, though it can be performed with a regional block, such as an epidural or even local anesthesia, for the truly brave woman. Mini-laps are still commonly performed, though recovery is slower and more painful than procedures in which a laparoscope is used, due to the larger incision.

Laparoscopy

Another abdominal approach to female sterilization requires the use of a laparoscope. Laparoscopy is the direct visualization of the abdominal cavity and tubes using a tiny telescope. Laparoscopy is a common surgical procedure that's generally done on an outpatient basis.

After the patient is under general anesthesia, the surgeon inserts a needle in the lower abdomen and injects carbon dioxide gas by means of an instrument that monitors pressure. Simply stated, a bubble of gas goes into the abdomen. Normally the abdominal organs push up against each other, so without the gas bubble, the surgeon can't see much. The anesthesiologist tips the patient's head down slightly so that the gas rises to the pelvis.

The laparoscope is thin enough for insertion through a small incision near the navel. The scope is equipped with a lens and a special attachment that transmits light through the tube. Through a second or third small incision at the pubic hairline, the surgeon inserts additional instruments to move structures, pick them up, or stabilize them for further observation.[3] After locating the fallopian tubes, the physician elevates each one. Electric current (which scars the tubes), clipping (which pinches the tubes shut), or a banding process (which constricts the tubes) can then be used to block each tube. Afterward, the scope and other instruments are removed from the abdominal cavity, and the small incisions are sutured and covered.

Hysteroscopic Approaches to Sterilization: Essure

Unlike the laparoscope, which goes through the abdomen for viewing the tubes from the outside, the hysteroscope goes inside the uterus and is used to view the tubes from within. Whereas with laparoscopic sterilization the tubes are cut, tied, or banded, hysteroscopic sterilization occurs by initiating a process in which the tubes are blocked by a scarring response.

Hysteroscopic sterilization, using fiberoptics to see and operate inside the uterus, was unimpressive until relatively recently. Such procedures, which began about thirty years ago, didn't reliably close the tube. And when a door is ajar, strangers—in this case persistent, relentless, adventurous sperm—can find their way in, wooed and wowed by the awaiting egg. Early efforts at various tubal plugs failed both to completely block the tube and to stay in place. The plugs would often fall out or pass in the menses, unknown to the unsuspecting (and soon-to-be pregnant) woman. Physicians tried cautery to electrically fuse the tubes. Yet often the result was still conception, with a higher risk of ectopic pregnancy. So for a while the approach was abandoned. But fairly recently another means of sterilization using hysteroscopic surgery has become available.

For the woman who loathes the thought of surgery—the hospital, the general anesthesia, the cutting, the stitches, the scarring, and the recovery—a relatively new procedure provides an alternative:

hysteroscopic sterilization using a microinsert device called Essure.[4] The U.S. government announced in late 2002 that it had approved Essure for female sterilization procedures.[5] The patient can now have surgery in a day hospital or an outpatient surgical center using local anesthesia with or without sedation, resulting in less anxiety and no scars. The entire process takes only a few hours and offers a quick return to normal activities.

In this procedure, the physician inserts the viewing scope (hysteroscope) up the vagina, through the cervix, and into the uterus. The doctor can thus see the inside of the uterus and both tubal openings (the tubal *ostia*, meaning "mouth" or "opening"). The image seen through the scope can be projected onto a TV screen or video monitor.

Having found the opening of the tube, the physician inserts a catheter with an Essure device, which looks like a tiny spring, up the vagina and into the uterus on a guide wire. An Essure coil, or microinsert, is placed at the opening of each fallopian tube. After the catheter is removed, the Essure device expands and remains in place in the tube. Imbedded in its coils is a mesh of Dacron-like material, used widely in medical procedures. The coil irritates the tube's lining, causing scar tissue to grow. Over time the scar tissue plugs the tube permanently. But there's the catch: over time—about three months. Immediately following the operation, the tube is still not sealed. It takes about three months for the woman's healing response to cause tissue to scar around the device, thus blocking the tube.

When approving Essure, the Food and Drug Administration cautioned that women must use another type of contraception during those three months. Then patients must return for testing to confirm that the scar tissue has fully blocked the tubes. Confirmation is done by shooting X-ray dye through the tubes. If the X-ray shows that no fluid has flowed out of the tubes, the patient is considered sterile.

The Essure procedure costs about the same as traditional tubal ligation—approximately twenty-five hundred dollars—and so far women who have had the procedure give it high marks for overall satisfaction. For obese patients and for those who've had abdominal surgeries, this procedure may be a better option than laparoscopy or a mini-lap. A disadvantage of the hysteroscopic approach is a higher risk of complications such as perforation of the uterus and hemorrhage. Also, some women pass out or have unusual heart rhythms when undergoing the procedure. In addition, the Essure approach requires special technical skills that many physicians lack. Further, in about one in ten patients the placement has failed, requiring another procedure. Candidates with histories of pelvic inflammatory disease make poor candidates, as do those with cervicitis, unexplained vaginal bleeding, suspicion of malignancy, an abnormal uterine cavity, abnormal tubes, or an allergy to nickel or iodine.[6]

How successful is Essure? Because the hysteroscopic approach is relatively new, we have no long-term data. However, the three-year data are excellent, with *no pregnancies reported*.[7] In fact, the procedure is so effective that it's unlikely the tube can ever be reopened. In vitro fertilization (IVF), which bypasses the tubes, would likely be needed should a patient want more children after having had hysteroscopic sterilization.

Uterine Ablation

Sometimes a patient has persistent abnormal bleeding that fails to respond to medicine. In such cases, her physician may recommend uterine ablation. This procedure involves destroying the uterine lining (endometrium) by using electric current, laser, or heated fluid. A patient who undergoes an ablation must be finished building her family because when effectively done, a uterine ablation makes it nearly impossible for the embryo to implant. Women who do conceive after ablation (about 1 percent) typically face high-risk pregnancies.[8]

If a woman is still ovulating when she has a uterine ablation, she should know that the possibility exists for fertilization. Without a healthy uterine implantation site, the developing embryo will either die or cause a high-risk pregnancy due to implantation in the tube or cornua (the place where the tube enters the uterus), clearly matters for concern. If your physician recommends uterine ablation and you're still ovulating, either use other means of contraception or ask about also having a tubal procedure done to prevent fertilization and the subsequent loss of life.

What about the risk factors associated with sterilization procedures? Whenever a patient has surgery (laparoscope, mini-lap, or hysteroscope), she faces risks. Complications associated with surgical sterilization include problems with anesthesia, hemorrhage, organ damage, and even death. Death is, of course, *exceedingly rare.* Also, occasionally during a tubal procedure, some of the blood vessels that supply the ovary are damaged. The resulting hormonal disruption has been known to cause abnormal menstrual patterns for a short time. Yet most women undergoing tubals are at the latter end of their reproductive years, so we expect to see some increase in menstrual irregularity and cramping anyway.

In addition, women between the ages of eighteen and thirty-nine who undergo a tubal ligation sterilization procedure *may* face an increased risk of developing ovarian cysts. These statistics are the results of one study of 392 women. While research tells us that of all the hormonal and nonhormonal methods of birth control, tubal sterilization has the greatest association with ovarian cysts, more research is needed to demonstrate an irrefutable link.[9]

PROS AND CONS OF SURGICAL CONTRACEPTION

Advantages
- "Permanent"
- Highly effective in preventing pregnancy
- No more need to think about contraception
- Decreased risk of pelvic inflammatory diseases
- Spontaneity restored in love life

Disadvantages
- High initial cost (unless done in conjunction with childbirth)
- Surgical procedure has associated risks
- Risk of tubal pregnancy
- Poststerilization regret

Sterilization Reversals

I would love to have another baby, so now I want a tubal reversal so I can try to get pregnant again.

I had my tubes tied almost six years ago after my fourth child. I regret that now. I don't think you should be able to sign the consent when you're pregnant and tired of being pregnant. I don't think I was thinking the way I would have been after the baby was born.

I got my tubal seven years ago exactly, and I regret it deeply now that my son is seven. I wish I'd have thought it through more carefully.

I am praying that the Lord would forgive me for getting a tubal and allow me to have that little girl that my husband and I have been praying for.

Once surgeons developed microtechniques for reversing sterilization procedures, many women requested reversals. In my own practice, I saw a number of patients who had permanent procedures done before age thirty. Having had four or five children in their early twenties, they couldn't imagine ever wanting more children. Then, whether through death or divorce, they lost a partner. After remarrying, they wanted another child. Remarriage is, in fact, one of the chief predictors of who will want reversals.[10]

Other patients had endured the deaths of one or more of their children and wanted more babies. Some had made decisions for sterilization when bowing to family pressure. Still others regretted their decisions on spiritual grounds.

Whatever their reasons, many women breathed sighs of relief upon learning that "permanent" did not necessarily mean "irreversible." So while the options for reversal are expensive, complicated, and offer no guarantee of a child, many patients try them. In fact, reversals for women have about an 80 percent success rate.

With the availability of in vitro fertilization (IVF), pregnancy can happen even after tubal sterilization or failed tubal reversals. Yet the IVF approach costs about fifteen thousand dollars per cycle, for a one-time shot at having about a 30 percent chance of conception.

Questions and Answers about Sterilization for Her

Question: Do you recommend having a laparascopic tubal right after delivery?

Answer: No. You can't safely do a laparoscopy then. The uterus is at the navel and fills up the space, so there's no room to work. The patient can have other sterilization procedures at that time, but not laparoscopy.

Question: Is it painful to have a laparoscopy?

Answer: The patient usually experiences moderate discomfort in the abdominal area, and occasionally she will feel significant shoulder pain. This is due to the carbon dioxide used to inflate her belly for visual exposure and to provide room to operate. Tylenol with codeine or another pain medicine of similar strength is usually sufficient to relieve the discomfort, which generally subsides within a few days.

Question: Will sterilization make me less feminine?

Answer: No. Sterilization won't make you less feminine. It also won't cause weight gain or make you grow facial hair. It won't decrease your sexual pleasure or cause menopause either.[11]

Question: Is it true that after you have a tubal, it'll kill your sex drive?

Answer: Many patients experience the opposite. The newfound freedom from fear of pregnancy brings an improvement in sexual responsiveness. For some women, the hormones may be out of kilter for a while, but libido usually returns once everything heals.

Question: Would you say more patients regret or are happy with the decision to be surgically sterilized?

Answer: Most couples are extremely happy with the decision over the long term. Most feel they've made a wise decision.

Question: So in your practice you didn't see a lot of regret?

Answer: Actually, no, I didn't. Most who decided on permanent sterilization continued to feel it was the best choice.

Question: Is it usually the wife, the husband, or both, who want sterility reversed?

Answer: Sometimes it's a joint decision. But in my experience, it was more often the wife who had misgivings. I've had one or two husbands say he's the one who wants it undone, but more often, she was the one with longings. She wanted to hold a baby again.

Question: Which is easier, a tubal reversal or a vasectomy reversal?

Answer: Generally it's easier to reverse a vasectomy than a tubal. Reversal of a vasectomy takes less time and requires local anesthesia rather than general. However, the amount of time that has passed since the vasectomy was done can be a factor in its success.

Question: Did you ever do tubals for women under thirty?

Answer: I never did them for women under twenty-five and was reluctant to do them for women under age thirty.

Question: When's the worst time to decide to have a tubal?

Answer: I've never known a patient in labor to want more children. Anytime you're under stress and duress is a bad time to make a major decision.

If the patient has carefully weighed the pros and cons of permanent sterilization and decides to have a tubal procedure, the freedom from fear of conception can be liberating. Many couples have reported a dramatic rise in frequency of intercourse and sexual satisfaction following this procedure. Contraception no longer drains the family budget. And there's no "stopping in the act."

At the beginning of this chapter, we told of Angela, who had tried just about every contraceptive method possible. It's been three years since she had her tubal ligation. She and her husband continue to be content with their family size and they love the fact that they no longer have the expense or hassle of contraception. They say that the only hindrances to spontaneous love are their "insane schedules" and "the fact that there are little ears listening down the hall."

LET'S TALK ABOUT IT

1. Do you feel certain that your family is complete? Does your spouse feel the same way?
2. Do you believe a decision to undergo a sterilization procedure would be the wisest choice in your situation?
3. After committing your decision to prayer, do you feel sterilization is the best option for you as a couple?
4. Read the next chapter. Then discuss the pros and cons of female sterilization and vasectomy for your own situation.
5. Which of the methods described here are best suited to your needs. Why?
6. What does your doctor recommend as the best option for you?
7. How old are you and what influence does age have on your decision-making process?

CHAPTER 11

HIS TURN

VASECTOMY

During my wife's third pregnancy, she suggested being sterilized at the time of delivery, but I said I thought I should be the one to have the procedure. By the time she got the okay from her doctor following delivery, I had healed from my vasectomy and my sperm count was right where we wanted it—at zero.

I get a rash after I use a condom, and I have burning and pain after we use a spermicide. A vasectomy could make life so much simpler.

For health reasons, my wife needs to avoid getting pregnant again. It's far easier for me to do something about that than it is for her.

A clamp here and a snip there, and it's over. No operating suite, no general anesthesia, no hospital bills. Less expensive, less complex, and less invasive than female sterilization, vasectomy is the most common approach to male sterilization. Worldwide, about 4 million men per year have vasectomies. About five hundred thousand of these are in the United States. That accounts for about 7 percent of American married couples.[1]

Vasectomy is the third most common form of contraception for married couples—the other two being tubal ligation and the pill. More than 80 percent of U.S. insurers cover vasectomy, which costs between three hundred fifty and twelve hundred dollars. In Canada, vasectomy is an insured service.[2]

Vasectomy is the surgical interruption of the vas deferens—the tube that carries sperm from the testicle to the seminal vesicles, or storage glands. Because the procedure can be performed using local anesthesia, vasectomy is commonly done in an urologist's office, though some general surgeons and family practice physicians perform vasectomies too.

For most men, a vasectomy is no big deal. Yet many men facing the procedure have admitted feeling self-conscious, concerned that the doctor and assistants (who often include female nurses) will scrutinize their anatomies. Some men experience heightened anxiety about being awake during the procedure.

I had a lot of apprehension about the procedure. I was frightened about the pain more than anything. But it's over now, and I am totally pleased.

After I arrived, the nurse took my blood pressure. It was high, thanks to my anxiety. I had taken two antianxiety pills and another when I got to the doctor's office. The nurse asked if I felt nervous and if the meds had helped. I said I still felt nervous, so she gave me a shot of Valium in the hip.

Wearing a hiked-up gown, the patient lies on the operating table. Part of his scrotal area is shaved, if necessary. The physician "scrubs" and puts on gloves while the patient is scrubbed and covered so that only a portion of the scrotum is exposed.

The surgeon palpates the scrotal area to find by feel both of the vas deferens, one at a time. After locating the first area for incision, the doctor numbs the appropriate area with a local anesthetic. Once it has taken effect, the patient may feel pressure or experience a slight tugging sensation, but he feels no pinching, poking, or cutting.

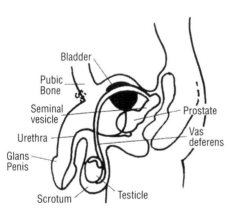

Bladder
Pubic Bone
Seminal vesicle
Urethra
Glans Penis
Scrotum
Prostate
Vas deferens
Testicle

The classic vasectomy procedure involves making a tiny incision. Then the doctor moves the vas up to the opening and reaches through with a small clamp to grab and gently pull the vas (or a small loop or bend of it) up through the incision. It can then be cut, tied, or clamped with a clip. Afterward the physician closes the incision with dissolvable stitches so the patient won't have to return to have the stitches removed. Some surgeons use a knifeless, or no-scalpel, procedure, which involves using needles and instruments inserted through a needle hole to complete the procedure, but many consider this more marketing hype than substance.

I'm totally afraid of needles and shots, but I hardly felt the shots. The entire operation lasted about forty-five minutes. Then the doctor helped me put on a special pair of support underwear, and I lay on the table for a few more minutes, then walked out. My legs felt a little rubbery, but I walked fine—and with no pain.

After the procedure, I went out to meet my wife. Our first stop was at the grocery store to get a few packs of frozen peas. Then we headed home to bed and peas on the boys. I relaxed, and before I knew it, I was asleep. I woke up about six hours later. No pain, no aches, and relieved it was over.

The only real pain I experienced was when my daughter jumped into my lap the next day.

After a vasectomy, in which part of the vas deferens is removed, the specimens are sent to a lab to confirm a successful operation. The pathology report confirms the successful completion of the procedure.

An alternative to having an incision is a "cut and block" done with a product called Vasclip. A device about the size of a rice grain, Vasclip blocks the flow of sperm. The clip can be inserted with a tiny introducer that looks like a needle but is a bit larger in diameter. The procedure takes about ten minutes and costs about three hundred fifty dollars.[3] Once long-term studies can show an effectiveness rating comparable with that of traditional vasectomy, ease of reversibility may make this technique the more popular.

Ice packs and Tylenol Plus with codeine or Darvocet can relieve any discomfort a man may have following a vasectomy. If no complications develop, such as bleeding or infection, a man who schedules a vasectomy for Friday can normally return to work on Monday unless his job requires heavy lifting or manual labor.

Vasectomy: The Three-Month Interval

The time between the procedure and the green light to resume relations is fairly short—a matter of days. Yet the time that must lapse before couples can rely on the procedure's contraceptive benefits is another matter. People may think, "Why a delay? Hasn't the 'stream' been cut off?" The answer is, "Yes, but . . ."

Imagine standing at the top of a mountain near a spring, the source of a stream downhill. At the bottom of the mountain, the stream feeds into a lake. If you built a dam up at the spring, it would cut off the stream's water source. Yet for a while, as far as anyone at the bottom of the mountain can tell, the stream will still flow as usual. It takes a while before the stream disappears.

The vasectomy is like the dam, and the male "lake" (the seminal vesicles) lies "downstream" from the "spring" (the testicles producing sperm). The inflow to the lake is dammed up, but the sperm are still available until the lake is dry. All the sperm already stored up—like the stream still flowing downhill between the spring and the lake after a dam has been built—must be emptied (ejaculated) before the procedure can be trusted for contraception. *A man is still fertile for about three months after the procedure, so couples should use alternate contraception.* A follow-up analysis of the ejaculate is recommended to verify that the sperm count is zero. Fewer than 1 percent of couples have a pregnancy after vasectomy if they've waited for a zero sperm count.

Side Effects: Fact or Fiction

Many people assume there will be no ejaculate following vasectomy. Yet that's not the case. A man who has had a vasectomy will still ejaculate seminal fluid; it's just devoid of sperm. Think of it as another stream feeding the reservoir, but this stream has no fish. The body does continue to make sperm, but they are absorbed by the bloodstream rather than exiting the body through the ejaculate.

Once a man heals from the tenderness caused by the incisions, he usually experiences few or no side effects. Yet one invisible side effect is the development of antisperm antibodies. These develop in about 60 percent of men following vasectomy. In short, a patient becomes allergic to his own sperm. That's because the sperm, which get "backed up" following surgery, must be absorbed by the body. And some of the "sperm parts" stimulate an immune response. But it's not an allergy like hay fever. Patients who have antisperm antibodies usually never know about it. As far as we know, the only problem associated with antisperm antibodies is if a man later wants his fertility restored. Antibodies are the body's fighter cells and the antisperm variety attack sperm as though they're an invading disease. This can severely impair future fertility by hampering sperm movement and vitality.[4]

While there has been ongoing concern about a connection between vasectomy and prostate disease or cancer, no scientifically significant link has been demonstrated.

I know some men think having a vasectomy will somehow make them "less of a man." This is complete rubbish, of course. Vasectomies don't change your hormone production (I'll go on producing testosterone), and they do nothing except eliminate sperm from your ejaculations. If you know you don't want children, is it manly to expect your wife to take pills every day or have a much more involved operation because you're scared of a simple, safe operation?

Vasectomy: Just the FAQs

When it comes to most issues associated with sexuality, myths abound. Here are some common questions about vasectomy, which will help you separate myth from fact.

Question: Is vasectomy 100 percent effective as a contraceptive method?

Answer: No method is foolproof, but vasectomy comes close. Surgical sterilization (his and hers procedures combined) has a pregnancy rate of about fourteen pregnancies per one thousand procedures. The cumulative pregnancy rate is 1.85 percent during a ten-year period.[5]

Question: Do I stop making sperm after a vasectomy? And if so, doesn't that affect my manhood?

Answer: Following vasectomy, the testes continue to produce sperm. Having nowhere to go, the sperm hit a dead end when they reach the clamp, cut, or pellet from the vasectomy, so sperm collect in the epididymis. Then they age and die. Normally the body breaks them down as it does dead cells in other parts of the body. Dead sperm are then absorbed into the bloodstream and eliminated. Sometimes people associate manhood with male hormone (testosterone) and sperm production, but this operation doesn't even make a dent in one's manhood.

Question: Will my erections feel the same as they did before the operation?

Answer: Yes. Vasectomy has no effect on erection or ejaculation. Virtually the same amount of semen or fluid is ejaculated as was present before the operation. The only difference is the absence of sperm.

Question: Will I still have an ejaculate, or will it be dry?

Answer: Neither you nor your partner will notice a change in the moisture or volume of the ejaculate.

Question: What if the knife slips? Is there a risk of impotence or even of losing important parts?

Answer: In the unlikely event that the knife should slip, it would cut through the vas and some scrotal fat, perhaps a tiny vessel or two. The penis isn't even in the operative field. Nor are the testicles near the incision. So while infection, bleeding, hematoma (collection of blood), and spontaneously restored fertility are remote possibilities, serious complications are exceedingly rare, as with most surgical procedures. A significant infection can destroy the testicles, decreasing libido and requiring hormone replacement, but that is a rare condition indeed.

Question: When am I considered sterile?

Answer: Following vasectomy, the patient needs to return to the doctor about six weeks to three months later to have his ejaculate analyzed. Some clinics use the guideline of analyzing the sperm count after fifteen ejaculations.

Couples with concerns about collecting the ejaculate for the sperm count via masturbation have several options. The wife can accompany her husband into the collection room to assist him. Or if his wife is not present, a husband can fill his mind with images of her, avoiding the lust issue that the Bible warns against. Another option is to obtain the sample at home (ironically, a glass baby-food jar is ideal for transporting the sample) before whisking it off to the laboratory. Specimens must be fresh on arrival at the laboratory, so advance arrangements must be made with the medical office.

Once the lab confirms a zero sperm count, the patient is sterile. Until then, backup contraception is strongly recommended. How long a couple must wait is dependent on the number of ejaculations a man has; the man having sex multiple times per week will empty the reservoir far faster than the man ejaculating twice monthly will.

Question: Can a vasectomy be reversed?

Answer: Yes, sometimes. About two in one thousand men who have vasectomies regret their decision and want reversals.[6] The main reasons for requesting a vasectomy reversal are remarriage, death of a child, or an improvement in finances followed by a wish for another child. Fewer than 10 percent of men who request reversals do so because of physical or psychological problems following vasectomy.[7]

Reversals are expensive and are not usually covered by insurance, so couples should avoid permanent sterilization unless they've fully and prayerfully considered all the ramifications. Pregnancy rates following vasectomy reversal range anywhere from 16 to 85 percent, depending on a variety of factors, including the ability of the surgeon, the way in which the original operation was performed, and the time that has lapsed since the vasectomy procedure.[8] The longer it has been since the original operation, the lower the odds of success, as antibodies have had more time to develop. Even if the pipeline is reconstructed (allowing sperm to be ejaculated again), if antisperm antibodies are present, they'll hinder conception.

Question: What will vasectomy do to my sex drive?

Answer: Vasectomy will not affect your sex drive unless you develop complications. There is certainly no physiological basis for erectile dysfunction or diminished libido associated with vasectomy. In fact, many couples report that once they know that the risk of unwanted pregnancy is behind them, they find greater freedom in their sexual expression. Most problems with erection and libido following vasectomy are psychological, not physical.

Question: I've heard it's painful to have a vasectomy. Is that true?

Answer: Pain is relative. But most guys do fine with uncomplicated vasectomy procedures. You may experience discomfort for the first few days following the procedure, but it's easily managed with medication.

Question: Will vasectomy increase my risk of cancer?

Answer: Prostate cancer affects one in six American men. All studies to date indicate that vasectomy is not a risk factor for prostate cancer, testicular cancer, or any other kind of cancer.

Question: Which is better, a tubal for her or a vasectomy for him?

Answer: The advantage is heavily on the side of vasectomy unless the wife opts for sterilization at the time of delivery. Cost, ease, and potential complication factors make vasectomy preferable to a tubal. If she's already in the hospital having an epidural or anesthesia with childbirth, then the tubal is a reasonable option. Still, generally speaking, tubal sterilization is a huge operation and is more expensive to reverse. It's about twenty times more likely than vasectomy to have major complications, costs three times as much, and is more likely to fail.[9]

To hear some guys tell it, having a vasectomy is a big deal. They may not show you the scar, but they'll tell you they went under the knife. But you cut yourself more than that when you nick yourself shaving.

Once they have the surgery, some guys think they have bragging rights. Vasectomy may be a good thing to do, but it's not up there with "heroic."

I got "fixed." Isn't that an interesting term? It worked before it got fixed, and now that it's fixed, it doesn't work. They really should call it "broken."

VASECTOMY: PROS AND CONS

Pros

- Outpatient
- Local, not general, anesthesia
- Cheaper than her tubal
- Quick recovery
- Can be done with small incision or special needle
- No more kids
- No more contraception
- Restoration of spontaneity, creativity
- No monitoring cycles, no watching mucus
- High degree of early reversibility

Cons

- Psychological impact for some
- Reversal less effective than with tubal procedures*
- Skittishness about surgery "there"
- Slight risk of infection, complications such as bleeding, hematoma

*If done before two years pass, vasectomy reversals are actually quite successful.

Having a vasectomy is a personal and important decision. A growing percentage of husbands, recognizing that vasectomy is generally much easier and less costly than tubal ligation, are making their way to the doctor's office for the procedure. Some men report that even though they feel good about their overall decision, there is a pang of sadness at the moment when the final analysis comes back confirming that they are sterile. But the overwhelming majority of these men also feel, as one husband expressed, that "it's just a momentary pang that disappears after that first celebratory unprotected sex."

LET'S TALK ABOUT IT

1. Do you feel certain that your family is complete? Does your spouse feel the same way?
2. Do you believe a decision to undergo a sterilization procedure would be the wisest choice in your situation?
3. After committing your decision to prayer, do you feel sterilization is the best option for you as a couple?
4. Read the previous chapter. Then discuss the pros and cons of female sterilization and vasectomy for your own situation.
5. Which of the methods described here are best suited to your needs? Why?
6. What does your doctor recommend as the best option for you?
7. How old are you and what influence does age have on your decision-making process?

CHAPTER 12

THE FUTURE OF CONTRACEPTION

Methods in Development for Him

In past decades, men and women alike tended to consider contraception the woman's responsibility. Consequently, researchers have long histories of focusing more on contraceptive options for women than for men. While we read that in ancient times, rubbing crushed juniper berries all over the male part before coitus prevented conception,[1] for years now, the entire male arsenal of contraceptive methods has consisted of withdrawal, condoms, and vasectomy—not exactly a wide range. A Kaiser Family Foundation survey done in the past few years found that attitudes have been shifting, however. Two-thirds of American men say they would take a male version of the pill. Yet a certain amount of skepticism still abounds. When good news about research on a male contraceptive pill was announced in 2003, headlines in Great Britain included, "Men on the pill? Yeah, right."[2]

> There are certain things you wouldn't trust a man with. You would not let a man pick what you were going to wear to an important function, for example, as he would have you looking either virginal or resembling a whore in distress. You would not put it to a man to decide how you should have your hair cut, or how you should decorate your house. . . . But the biggest thing you would not trust a man with is contraception.[3]

Despite such skepticism, attitudes toward contraception have definitely shifted. Today most couples who use contraception consider prevention of pregnancy a shared responsibility.

Prevailing attitudes have not been the only reason for the relative slowness in developing male contraceptives. Researchers have found convenient, reversible, affordable approaches difficult to develop because of the male anatomy. The male storage system creates a lag time of two to three months from sperm production in the testicles to delivery via ejaculation. Thus, what a man does today won't alter his fertility for quite some time. In a society in which we tap our feet as we wait for dinner to warm in the microwave, few people want to plan so far ahead—especially when it comes to sex. Yet couples in committed, monogamous relationships have the luxury of such long-term planning.

Still, what's taking so long? Why don't we have a male contraceptive pill yet? While few doubt that a male pill would be extraordinarily successful (more than 100 million women use daily oral contraceptives, resulting in huge profits for pharmaceutical companies), basic biology is partly responsible for the delay. In addition to the three-month lag time for men, oral contraceptive pills (OCPs) for women work by suppressing one egg per month; the male version will require suppressing millions of sperm and doing so every day of the month.

A further reason for the delay is the difficulty in getting medications approved by the Food and Drug Administration. Pharmaceutical executives still feel skittish, especially after what happened with Norplant, which was hailed as the best thing since the pill, only to be removed from the market after women filed lawsuits claiming the manufacturer failed to fully inform them about side effects.[4]

The Male Pill

Researchers in fourteen centers throughout Europe are conducting one of the largest trials ever of the male pill.[5] But don't hold your breath; this one could still take a while. As with women on OCPs, men using the male pill in clinical trials are experiencing side effects. These involve a variety of problems including liver damage, prostate problems, and the worst insult of all, gynecomastia.[6] (What man wants a contraceptive method that makes him grow breasts?)

When are they going to release a male birth control pill? As my dad always says, it's better to unload a pistol than to wear a bulletproof vest.

I've heard the male pill makes testicles become smaller. Call me a male pig, but I don't want my testicles shrinking.

I participated in one of the trials for the male pill. The only change I noticed was increased libido. From my point of view, it had a positive side effect.

Chinese researchers are developing a male contraceptive pill that they hope will not only prevent conception but also protect against sexually transmitted infections (STIs). Their pill targets a natural antibacterial chemical involved in sperm production and storage, a substance found in rats that seems to have equivalents in humans and chimps.[7] But we won't see that product anytime soon either.

Still, some good options for men are on the horizon. While the following may not be in pill form, a few methods offer promise for male contraception with few negative effects.

Just Shoot Me: Progestin DMPA Injection

A team of Australian researchers gave men progestin DMPA (depot medroxyprogesterone acetate) in injectable form quarterly for one year. Progestin DMPA is the same as Depo-Provera, used in contraception for women. In men, the hormone stops sperm production. In this study, none of the participants' partners conceived, and all of the men had normal fertility a few months after stopping treatment.[8]

Other research is proceeding with a different pituitary hormone, prolactin, which we normally associate with the production and release of breast milk in nursing mothers. In men, prolactin blocks production of the hormone LH (luteinizing hormone), thus decreasing the sperm count.

So far both methods have a big drawback: testosterone levels plummet. So patients have to add testosterone shots or skin implants to the regimen to maintain their sexual health. Side effects associated with replacement testosterone have included headaches, nausea, and vomiting. But the other expected side effects of these male contraceptives, such as mood swings and lowered sex drive, did not occur. Still, considering the complications, researchers estimate it will be years, not months, before we see a male contraceptive method that safely takes a sperm count from millions to zero.[9]

The Drug That Shugged Me: The Shug

The Shug is like a tiny stopper surgically placed inside a man's body. A silicone double plug with nylon tails, the Shug blocks sperm from getting through the vas deferens. Yet the Shug is less permanent than a vasectomy, and it requires no hormones, ongoing shots, pills, or spermicides. Spontaneity rules.

Rather than using a scalpel, with its accompanying risk of scarring, the physician can inject the Shug into the vas deferens using a needle and anchor it in place with a small suture. The plug is no larger than the internal diameter of the vas. A man could, theoretically, have a Shug removed and replaced several times over the course of his lifetime. And when the plug is in, it works. Yet one side effect may be the development of antisperm antibodies. Because the sperm are "dammed up" with this method, the body must absorb them, which may trigger an immune response. Such a response could grow in significance over years of use, impairing future fertility by hampering sperm movement and vitality.[10]

The Sperminator: RISUG

Reversible Inhibition of Sperm Under Guidance, better known as RISUG (pronounced RICE-ugh), was invented thirty years ago when a scientist looking for a way to purify drinking water stumbled onto a way to make a male contraceptive.[11] Mostly being investigated overseas, RISUG uses a substance called styrene maleic anhydride.[12] RISUG involves injecting a compound into each vas deferens, the exit ramps from the testes for sperm. The compound in RISUG coats the inner wall of the ducts with a gel that has a negative and a positive electric charge. RISUG effectively renders sperm incapable of fertilizing an egg by rupturing the sperms' delicate membranes as they pass through the ducts.

In five minutes it was over, and I went home feeling fine. My wife was planning to get a tubal, but I persuaded her to let me get the RISUG injection instead. We have four children and she's tired. An operation would not have been good for her.

Now I'm electrically charged.

If RISUG is for real, I think the number of men forced to choose between a little shot in the privates versus no sex will explode like with Viagra. I just hope it's true and it happens.

RISUG may be superior to vasectomy in a number of ways. First, it doesn't block anything but instead renders sperm powerless. Thus, researchers see none of the antibody problems associated with blockage. Second, RISUG is easily reversible. By flushing out the gel, doctors can quickly restore fertility. Third, it requires no snipping or clipping, causing some men to say, "Uh-huh! I'm da man. I can do this!"

Studies of men conducted for more than eight years have demonstrated no increase in prostate problems with RISUG, which has completed phase I and phase II trials in India.[13]

Sperm with Attachment Disorder: Nifedipine

After infertility specialists noticed that a disproportionately high number of their male patients took nifedipine to treat high blood pressure or migraines, researchers began investigating the effect of the medication on fertility. They learned that the drug's calcium channel blockers affect sperm cell membranes. The result: sperm are unable to attach themselves to the outer wall of a wooing egg. Nifedipine also interferes with enzymes that enable sperm to penetrate the egg. No attachment and no penetration means—*voilà!*—no fertilization.

While nifedipine has been on the market for twenty years, it remains untested and thus unapproved for contraceptive use, so its safety is unknown. Also, pharmaceutical companies may hesitate to advertise nifedipine as a contraceptive. Who wants to publicize that they might have unknowingly contributed to some patients' infertility problems?

What's Cooking? Gossypol

For generations the Chinese have cooked with cottonseed oil, which is inexpensive and plenteous. When a high number of Chinese men developed fertility problems, the government began researching a chemical in the oil as a possible contraceptive agent. The experimentation involved ten thousand subjects over ten years. Researchers concluded that gossypol (who came up with that name?) provided reliable contraception.

Taken orally in tablet form, gossypol doesn't upset male hormones.[14] But it has turned out to be less reversible than hoped. In fact, reversibility is the single biggest issue with gossypol. While gossypol use has not appeared to result in permanent loss of fertility, many men have continued to have low sperm counts long after discontinuing the medication. In fact, the period during which they had low sperm counts after discontinuing gossypol lasted longer than the period during which they took the pills. And the longer that men used gossypol, the longer their period of infertility lasted. Some men never regained normal sperm counts. As many as a fourth of the men remained infertile a year after stopping the medication.

In addition, between 1 and 10 percent of the men suffered from low potassium levels, leading to fatigue, weakness, kidney failure, irregular heart rhythms, and even paralysis. When giving the subjects extra potassium failed to overcome the effects, the study was discontinued in China. Brazilians, however, continued with trials using a lower dose of gossypol (which they called "Nofertil"). Still, the medication didn't make it to market.

Worldwide interest continues, however, because gossypol (or Nofertil) is inexpensive and readily available.

Methods in Development for Her

While men's contraceptive options have been relatively limited, women have had an enormous variety of contraceptive choices. And a few more appear to be around the corner.

In the past few years, researchers have discovered that the amount of carbohydrate on the uterine wall affects how early-stage embryos implant. As a result, some researchers plan to develop nonhormonal contraceptives that work by blocking embryo implantation—an option we find unethical.

Sealing the Tubes Chemically: Quinacrine

Quinacrine changed my life! The procedure was essentially pain-less, affordable, and freeing! I love my new lifestyle.

One rather controversial approach to nonsurgical permanent sterilization that is still being investigated involves the application of quinacrine, a medication no longer manufactured in the United States. Quinacrine was used for decades to treat malaria. In the past twenty-four years, more than one hundred thirty thousand women in thirty-one countries have undergone sterilization procedures that involve the use of quinacrine pellets.[15]

The use of quinacrine as a contraceptive has been introduced in the United States but is not in widespread use. The physician uses an intrauterine device (IUD) applicator to insert pellets directly into the uterus once a month for two consecutive months. The tablets dissolve within about half an hour. In the weeks that follow, a massive amount of scar tissue forms, blocking sperm from entering the tubes to meet the egg.

Quinacrine is a low-cost alternative to female sterilization and is being used in India, Chile, and other parts of the world. So far it appears to be safe. It is too soon to tell about any long-term effects such as cancer risk or risk of ectopic pregnancy.

Some patients have complained of headache, light bleeding, abdominal pain, vaginal itching, and a yellow discharge following quinacrine insertion. The medication does not, however, appear to cause major infections.

Sealing the Tubes Chemically: Erythromycin

A similar approach uses erythromycin for nonsurgical steriliza-tion. The use of erythromycin, however, has a somewhat storied his-tory. India banned its use for female sterilization in 1998, amid doubts about its safety and in response to a petition by activists after the medication had been used in the illegal sterilization of more than thirty thousand Indian women.[16]

Doctors place pellets of erythromycin, an antibiotic, at the upper part of the uterine cavity. Both quinacrine and erythromycin, when placed in the womb, cause scar tissue, which blocks the fallopian tubes. Erythromycin seems safe but has an unacceptably high failure rate of 28 to 35 percent.[17] A study published in 2000, however, indicated that erythromycin was more effective in preventing pregnancy than quinacrine.[18]

The risk of ectopic pregnancy with these methods still requires further study.

Where We Are Now

Despite brilliant minds and plenty of research dollars devoted to developing new approaches to contraception, a survey of what's ahead in the near future includes nothing revolutionary. At the same time, the number of couples delaying childbearing is on the rise. In fact, in the United States, the age of parents at the time of their first child's birth is now higher than it has ever been. Young couples now expect access to methods of contraception that have no associated health risks yet allow for absolute sexual spontaneity. And they want methods that are "natural," which they perceive to be more healthful. Ten years ago you wouldn't have found salad listed on the menus at most fast-food joints. But in our increasingly health-conscious society, we now find fresh garden greens next to the listings of french fries and double cheeseburgers with high-fat sauce. So when it comes to our contraceptives, we want perfect effectiveness ratings. All this and FDA approval too.

We still don't have a male pill. Nor has anyone found a foolproof way to make the human egg impenetrable. We've come a long way from crocodile dung and burlap with a bow, but we still have a way to go before we'll be able to send sperm into hibernation on demand or make ovulation cease by willing it so.

LET'S TALK ABOUT IT

1. Considering all you've read, which (if any) of the methods of contraception discussed in this chapter would you consider using, and which are out of the question?

2. Rank the following in order of importance for you. Have your spouse do the same and then compare notes.
   - Absence of an abortifacient effect
   - Effectiveness
   - Cost
   - Ease of use
   - Accessibility
   - Absence of hormonal alterations to the body
   - Concern about long-term risks
   - Degree of reversibility

PART 3

WE ARE FAMILY

CHAPTER 13

UNLESS THE LORD BUILDS THE HOUSE . . .

W e've considered the available contraceptive options and some that are on the horizon. Some are unreliable, others quite reliable. Some are temporary, some permanent. Some are reversible, some aren't. The so-called permanent options require more deliberation and soul-searching than do spermicides and barrier methods. Yet any decision about contraception should involve consideration of the spiritual implications that might influence a couple's choices.

The Blueprint

Jesus said, "Suppose one of you wants to build a tower. Will he not first sit down and estimate the cost to see if he has enough money to complete it?" (Luke 14:28). As an economist once said, "There are two kinds of people in this world: those who divide everything into two groups, and those who don't."[1] When it comes to family planning, many people get categorized into rigid groupings. Those with big families get pitted against those who stress planning well. Those who emphasize obeying "be fruitful and multiply" get pitted against those who focus on "have dominion" as it relates to the conservation of the earth. Yet often the issues may not be as black and white as they might seem.

The world around us reveals the wisdom of God's design in creating a woman and a man joined in marriage to create a family. Having considered the specifics of conception and contraception, we now turn to think about the context in which such decisions are made: the family. It's vitally important that as part of this discussion, we consider the blueprint for families. God's Word provides such a blueprint, and biblical considerations are foundational to our thinking about contraception and family building.

This important chapter comes late in the book because we recognize and appreciate that most people buying a book about contraception want to get down to the specifics pretty quickly. Once their initial questions have been addressed, however, it's important to think about deeper foundational issues before following any course of action.

Let's Start at the Very Beginning

When children enter the world, they do so within a relational context—hopefully within a family. Ideally they have active, involved parents, both mother and father, who are married to each other. Kids in two-parent households say no to drugs more often than kids in single-parent homes. With fathers actively involved in their lives, children are less likely to get in trouble with the law, drop out of school, get pregnant as unwed teenagers, or be at increased risk for mental health problems. Even children with divorced parents usually do better when parents share joint custody than when the kids interact with only one parent.[2] When families are strong, society benefits.

What does *family* mean? Does it include husband and wife only? Or are children a necessary component? If so, how many? Can there be too few or too many? Is a family incomplete or abnormal without children or without a certain number of children? Are children a promised blessing to those who live in obedience to God's commands?[3] Is a family incomplete prior to a couple's having children? Is a family diminished after the children are grown and gone? These questions require a careful look at the biblical record.

The First Family

Under the Spirit's inspiration, Moses recorded in Genesis the creation of the first family. There we discover that God made *both* male and female in his own image: "So God created man in his own image, in the image of God he created him; male and female he created them" (Gen. 1:27; see also Gen. 5:2).

While You Were Sleeping

To get the full picture of the first family, we need to also read Genesis 2:18–25. There we find a more detailed account of how God brought the first couple together. On each day of creation, God looked at what he'd made and declared it good. That is, until he created man from the ground. After he formed the man, God looked at his creation and declared, "It is *not good* for man to be alone" (v. 18, italics ours). Then he did something to improve the situation: "So the LORD God caused the man to fall into a deep sleep; and while he was sleeping, he took one of the man's ribs and closed up the place with flesh. Then the LORD God made a woman from the rib he had taken out of the man, and he brought her to the man. The man said, 'This is now bone of my bones and flesh of my flesh; she shall be called "woman," for she was taken out of man'" (vv. 21–23).

Finally God had sent the man a creature that was like him. After God made the woman and brought the man and woman together, he pronounced all things "very good" (1:31).

The text goes on to describe the woman as a "helper suitable" (2:18). This phrase is the translation of two Hebrew words that paint a beautiful picture of woman as a wonderful complement, companion, and partner. Rather than being man's apprentice, she helped him from a position of strength. "Helper" is the same word often used in Scripture to describe how God helps humans on the battlefield. Woman was man's indispensable companion.

God designed men and women with relational needs, the primary relational need being intimacy with God. And in the earthly sphere in the pre-sin state, the marriage union must have completely met the need for human relationship.

That first family consisted of two people. The words "bone of my bones and flesh of my flesh" carry the idea of being blood relatives, although spouses nowadays are not biologically related. Somehow, in a mysterious, miraculous way, God has joined husband and wife together.

Families reveal an important part of the person of God. We know from an overview of the entire Bible that God himself exists in community, in three persons having one nature—the interdependent Father, Son, and Holy Spirit. When the human family, biological or spiritual, operates as God intended, it reflects the mutuality of the Trinity.

Throughout Scripture, we see the concept of family used to convey a picture of our relationship with the infinite, eternal God. The prophet Hosea and his unhappy marriage parallels God and his relationship with Israel. Christian believers call one another brothers and sisters in the Lord. Jesus is called the bridegroom, and the church, his radiant bride. We read in Ephesians 5 that God designed earthly marriage to reflect a heavenly relationship. He ordained marriage and has blessed the family from the beginning.

Since God's creation of the first couple, human families have come in various shapes and sizes. Every individual since that time has been part of a physical family whose genealogy originates from that first orchard. Not everyone knows—and certainly not everyone *enjoys*—his or her parents. But whether someone comes from a large or small family, has joined that family through adoption or high-tech infertility treatment, was wanted or unwanted, each individual is part of the same genetic stream. We are all related in some way.

Multiplication 101

After creating the man and woman, God gave them a couple of directives: "God blessed them and said to them, 'Be fruitful and increase in number; fill the earth and subdue it. Rule over the fish of the sea and the birds of the air and over every living creature that moves on the ground'" (Gen. 1:28).

Often we notice that God told the man and woman to multiply, but we fail to see the *two* parts in his instructions: procreation *and* dominion, or rule. While we think of pregnancy as requiring both a man and a woman, we may overlook the fact that God has involved both man and woman in dominion, or co-ruling, over the earth.

We note that the command to multiply and rule is not repeated in the New Testament. So we wonder, was that task intended only for Adam and Eve, for all couples within the context of the old covenant, or for all couples for all time?

Many people believe the Genesis text implies that all married couples in every age have a moral duty to have as many children as possible. Some would even hold that *the* purpose of marriage is to procreate. Some have even gone so far as to specify that it's not just the children that are desired but, specifically, male children. Consider the words of a Christian scholar written within the last fifty years: "As in most ancient societies the real purpose of marriage is the procreation of lawful sons."[4]

Marriage Has Its Purposes

Is it true that the real purpose of marriage is procreation? To find out, let's consider the Scriptures we've just read. The first snapshot suggests that God's ultimate purpose in designing marriage was to reveal his own image (Gen. 1:26; Gen. 5:1–2). Second, the woman was God's solution to the man's being alone, so another purpose for marriage was companionship. Third, marriage brought completeness. When the man was by himself, God pronounced that what he had created was "not good," whereas after the woman came on the scene, God pronounced the couple together as "very good." Each of these pictures appears *before* God tells the man and woman to multiply. It's interesting that the mention of procreation is absent in the Genesis 2 account—a significant omission. One might expect that if procreation were a moral mandate and the sole purpose of marriage, reproducing would at least be mentioned where the details of the first couple's creation are first recorded.

So marriage appears to have several purposes. Other purposes for marriage surface in the New Testament, but at this point we'll limit ourselves to the text at hand. Certainly, part of God's design for marriage included procreation, but based on the Genesis text, it is not the *only* purpose.

The Birds and the . . . Fish?

Scroll back a bit further in Genesis to prehuman history and consider what happened on the fifth day of creation. God has just made sea creatures and birds and pronounced them good. And he gives some instructions: "God blessed them and said, 'Be fruitful and increase in number and fill the water in the seas, and let the birds increase on the earth'" (Gen. 1:22).

At this point the humans have yet to be created. But God's words to the creatures are identical to what he will tell the man and woman, except for the part about ruling. Did God *command* the animals to obey? No scholars we've found have argued that the fish or fowl were rational creatures that heard and obeyed a moral imperative to reproduce. (Imagine trout being pressured by others in their school to pick up the pace of spawning, or a chicken bragging about her egg production.) Instead, some scholars view "be fruitful and multiply" as a blessing and an authorization or acknowledgment of the creatures' ability to fulfill this function. In other words, this "blessing" meant God gave creatures the *capacity* to do what he wanted them to do as part of the fullness of life on earth. There is no sense of "have to" in the directive. Are we to assume that the same words given to two different groups had different meanings? That is, the animals *get to* procreate, but the humans *have to* procreate? Humans have a higher purpose in procreation than do the animals: we share in the divine work of creating human life and passing on the divine image. And as a race, we collectively share responsibility for filling and managing the earth.

The Empty Nest

The passage ends with an interesting observation: "For this reason a man will leave his father and mother and be united to his wife, and they will become one flesh" (Gen. 2:24). Some people have interpreted this as a command to the man to leave his parents as he initiates the marital relationship. Some have even seen it as a command that couples should not live with their in-laws. But that is not how listeners in Old Testament times would have heard it.

The words often translated "for this reason" signal a description ("that's why") rather than a prescription ("he must"). In other words, it's a description of what generally happens to a young man establishing a new family. Many a parent has been baffled over a son's or a daughter's easily transferred loyalties from the original family to a new spouse. How can their young person so easily choose the new love over a long-established relationship?

Here's why: because of God's design for that powerful "man-woman thing." While still part of their larger families, the new couple will go on to form a priority family unit that begins with their marriage.

We also read in this text that the man and woman were naked and unashamed (Gen. 2:25). This suggests purity in their sexuality and its full expression. Maleness and femaleness were part of the creation plan, and "they felt no shame" has a moral connotation in the ideal world of the garden. The distinction seems to extend beyond merely reproductive capability. There is a sense in which transparency, vulnerability, and trust are also present here. The man's and woman's differences were by God's design. Together they were "very good."

But then . . . the music changes as the dance is exchanged for a dirge. The man and woman choose to sin and are driven from the garden. All of creation groans. The couple struggles to rule not only the earth but also each other. Weeds will choke off good growth. And something else will happen.

When outlining the consequences of sin in the Garden of Eden, God told the woman that he would multiply her pain in bringing forth children (Gen. 3:16). We know he means physical pain here, but more than that is implied (literally, "your pain and your conception"). The whole process has broken down before it even had a chance to get started. The couple's two responsibilities—to be fruitful and to subdue the earth—now involve painful processes. He will sweat to work the earth; she will have pain in childbearing.

After leaving the garden, Adam and Eve live east of Eden. They do procreate, and their firstborn kills his brother. Before long, the entire world is so full of evil that God has to destroy it with a flood.

Then after Noah emerges from his voyage with the animals, we find an echo of the imperative to be fruitful and multiply (Gen. 9:1). Yet this time, the "fill and subdue" messages are absent, though a dread of humankind falls on the animal kingdom.

Yet notice what the pronouncement to Noah has in common with the one given to the first couple. In both cases, God's instructions to fill the earth come at critical junctures when those hearing the directives were earth's *only* human inhabitants.

First Adam and Eve are charged with increasing from two to many. Then, following the flood, Noah and his wife, along with six family members, face a similar task. They will begin the process and participate in it without completing it. (Though, interestingly, we do not see Noah having more offspring with his wife.)

The Family in Old Testament Times

Time passes. The earth is populated. And God gives the law through Moses. In his writings, we see descriptions of families in ancient cultures. At that point the concept of family is presented in biological terms. Parents thought in terms of interdependence. The family included all living generations, usually all living on the same property. And the heritage, or inheritance, would pass to the eldest male—that is, he would receive a double portion compared to the inheritance of his siblings. Rather than being "patriarchal" (each father ruling his own, separate household) as some have described it, it was more "patricentric." That is, the oldest father and his primary wife functioned together in their responsibilities, operating like the hub of a wheel. Each son with his wife and children formed a connected subunit, usually geographically connected on one family compound. Upon the patriarch's death, the central honor shifted to his eldest son.[5] The concept of family in Old Testament times (and in some parts of the world today) included all the male descendants of a living patriarch, along with their spouses.

In Old Testament times, people understood "family" to mean something much different from our present-day "nuclear family," which typically consists of a dad, a mom, 2.3 kids, and their pets. Twenty-first-century North American parents see their job as fostering independence, raising children, and sending them out into the world. Today parental goals often include providing a good education for one's children, who will then have the credentials or skills to go out and make it on their own. This goal would have been foreign to the people in Old Testament times.

Are Large Families the Ideal for Everyone and for Always?

The value of having large numbers of children in the cultures of Old Testament days is obvious. The infant-mortality and premature-death rates were very high. And those with larger landholdings needed more "hands" to work and defend their property. If the primary wife was unable to bear children, especially sons, additional wives were often added to the family to bear more children. While never prescribed or even commended in the Old Testament, polygamy is also never clearly condemned. God's ideal for the family was revealed later as one man and one woman until death separated them (Titus 1:6; 1 Cor. 7:39), but under Old Testament law, apparently allowances were made.

In the ancient Near East, villagers had no concept of social security, 401(k) plans, nursing homes, health insurance, or pensions. Instead, they had children. And when it came to warfare or defense, sons were primary. So a premium was placed on boys. This perspective on warfare is key to understanding the blessing of the "quiver" mentioned in Psalm 127—a chapter often quoted as reflecting God's ideal for large families in today's culture:

> Yes, sons are a gift from the LORD,
> the fruit of the womb is a reward.
> Sons born during one's youth
> are like arrows in a warrior's hand.
> How happy is the man who fills his quiver with them!
> They will not be put to shame
> when they confront enemies at the city gate.
> —Psalm 127: 3–5 NET

While some translators—perhaps in an effort to be gender inclusive—have chosen to go with "*children* are a gift," (Ps. 127:3 NASB, italics ours), a more precise rendering would be "sons are an inheritance." The psalmist seems to have in view a picture of economics and safety, which in his day depended on sons. The idea of physical defense is behind the reference to arrows, quivers, and enemies.

Picture the Old West when Native Americans used bows and arrows to fight. The quiver was the pouch in which warriors stored their arrows. Psalm 127 suggests that having a full quiver—that is, having many sons—was good. Certainly, if you ran out of arrows in the midst of a battle, or even on a hunt, you were in deep trouble.

The main point here isn't about having lots of sons and daughters. Sons were the means to an end. As "arrows," they provided protection in a world in which families, rather than police, enforced the law. In present-day North America, most people who have no children still have many, if not all, of the blessings the psalmist had in mind when he penned Psalm 127.

We see the overarching message of this psalm to be that the Lord is the blesser of our efforts and the protector and defender of our old age. All of our labors, including the labor to have and raise children, are exercises in futility without God's provision. We are blessed to live in a society in which as we grow increasingly brittle, we—with or without children—generally live without fear of starvation or harm.

The Times They Are A-Changin'

Psalm 127 was written at a time when virtually no one—man or woman—remained single. Compare that with our society today:

- Eighty-six million adults in the United States today are unmarried.
- Singles constitute more than 40 percent of the adult population in the nation.
- In many major metropolitan areas, singles comprise the majority of the adult population.
- The Census Bureau estimates that about 10 percent of adults will never marry.
- Married couples with minor children make up fewer than 25 percent of the nation's households.[6]

Most of us today would define family as an independent unit. We tend to envision the norm as families living more independently, in their own homes, remote from their parents. Once the children establish their own homes, they remain part of the former family, but in a new relationship—mostly independent, but also somewhat interdependent.

Scripture describes life in a much different cultural setting. So we must avoid taking its ancient poetry and narratives and applying them directly as commands in a completely different cultural context.

While we see an emphasis on biological families in the Old Testament, we do see hints that there's more to life than having kids. In the Wisdom Literature, we find foolish sons causing grief to their mothers (Prov. 10:1) and fathers (Prov. 17:25). More positively, Isaiah mentions that leaving an eternal legacy will be better for some than having children (Isa. 56:4–5). So while the Old Testament speaks primarily about biological reproduction and family units, we find subtle references to the importance of spiritual reproduction.

Fast-Forward to New Testament Times

That subtlety disappears when we come to the New Testament. The emphasis clearly shifts from physical reproduction to spiritual reproduction. In the New Testament, "family" is introduced as a metaphor for a spiritual community.

Spreading the gospel of Jesus Christ is elevated in the New Testament, even if it requires remaining single (1 Cor. 7:7). This is not meant to diminish the blessing of biological family and childbearing. But it reminds us that the church's main purpose is to live for God's glory and in relationship with him.

In the New Testament, intimacy with God is regularly pictured by drawing analogies to earthly familial relationships. Jesus loved children and spoke affectionately of them, and he taught about the childlike faith that adults should emulate. In his recorded discourses, Christ never commanded biological reproduction (though he clearly anticipated the survival of the race until his return). His emphasis was on kingdom growth and spiritual maturity. Careful study of the Beatitudes (Matt. 5:3–12) reveals the blessedness of spiritual poverty, hungering and thirsting after righteousness, and purity of heart among other things, with an expectation of persecution for faithful discipleship. Clearly, we are to see that abundant life consists of dimensions other than biological reproduction.

Anna (mentioned in Luke 2:36) was a righteous woman who never had children. And Aquila and Priscilla, Paul's married coworkers, don't appear to have had children. If they did, their offspring are not mentioned. So we find a variety of family photos in God's album of righteous people.

In John's writings (1 John 2), we find family relationships—spiritual children, youth, and fathers—used as metaphors for spiritual maturity. In Ephesians 5:22–23, Paul explains the mystery—something undiscoverable without the revelation of God—of marriage. He reveals that an essential purpose in God's joining of bride and groom is to provide an earthly picture of the heavenly union of Christ and the church. Ideally, then, even before children come and after they have grown, the union of husband and wife pictures the intimacy of relationship that Christ has with believers.

All of this reminds us that God's ultimate purpose for each person is not finite and temporal, but spiritual and eternal. We find hints of this spiritual priority in other Scriptures. Consider Paul's words to the Philippians: "To live is Christ and to die is gain" (Phil. 1:21). Paul saw a purpose in life that was greater than procreation. Two chapters later, he says that his life goal is to know Christ, and he counts everything else as "rubbish" in comparison (3:8).

If Paul was married—and there is a good chance that he was at some point—he never mentioned having any children. John the Baptist never married. Nor did Jesus. In fact, we read the following words of Jesus: "For there are some eunuchs who were that way from birth, and some who were made eunuchs by others, and some who became eunuchs for the sake of the kingdom of heaven. The one who is able to accept this should accept it" (Matt. 19:12 NET).

In Luke 14:26, we read other words from Jesus: "If anyone comes to me and does not hate his father and mother, his wife and children, his brothers and sisters—yes, even his own life—he cannot be my disciple." Jesus is not speaking here of cruel hate. Rather, he's stressing in relative terms that anything, including children, that takes preeminence over obedience to him is idolatry.

None of this should discourage anyone from having children. Our point is only that Scripture reminds us that our primary focus must be to seek first God's kingdom (Matt. 6:33). Consider a large family—the couple with eight children, who devote their lives to training those sons and daughters to love Christ. Consider a smaller family—the couple with two kids, who raise their children while going to language school in preparation for mission work in a third-world country. From the outside, someone without all the details might critically judge either one. Yet both may be living in response to the conviction of God's calling on their lives.

The Value of Human Life

While some people have overemphasized the importance of families over eternal priorities, at the other end of the spectrum is the tendency of many in our world to devalue children. One of the methods most commonly used worldwide to control family size and spacing is abortion, the willful destruction of human life.

Abortion as Contraception

Globally, between sixty million and one hundred million abortions are performed each year. In North America, we have averaged more than one million elective abortions yearly since the *Roe v. Wade* decision in 1973. Significant to our discussion, nearly one-fifth of abortions in the United States are performed on married women.[7] And in a 2003 report that included thirty-seven states and New York City, nearly 44 percent of abortions performed in 2000 were repeat abortions. Eighteen percent of women electing abortion reported having previously had two or more abortions, and in Maryland, the state with the highest repeat rate, 16.7 percent of abortion patients had already had three or more.[8] The rate of repeat abortions rose steadily between 1970 and 1990, but it appears to have leveled off. Abortion is common in many nations around the world, and we in the United States are no exception. We have destroyed a significant percentage of an entire generation. Many people rely on abortion as either a primary or a secondary means of contraception. Note the number of repeat abortions:

- 1973: 20 percent of abortions
- 1987: 44 percent of abortions
- 1995: 45 percent of abortions
- 2000: 44 percent of abortions[9]

Having lectured about the sanctity of human life in the Commonwealth of Independent States (CIS, or the former Soviet Union), I had occasion to learn from a number of gynecologists that abortion has been even more common there than it has been stateside. Married women often had five or more abortions during their childbearing years because no other contraceptive techniques were available. Not until the late 1980s did the number of Russian women using contraceptives exceed the number who used abortion to prevent births. Even when contraceptive techniques were available, which often they were not, they were too expensive for the average person to afford. At one time in the not too distant past, the cost for a month's supply of pills was equivalent to the average monthly salary. Many of my obstetrical colleagues in the CIS lamented that the government required them to perform abortions regardless of their personal beliefs.

Contraception and Devaluing Life

It has often been said that the availability of contraceptives in America has led to a mentality that devalues life, resulting in a higher abortion rate. Yet as the statistics in Russia have demonstrated, the *absence* of accessible contraceptives has also driven up the abortion rate.

It's wrong to take a human life. We believe each human, from the moment of fertilization, is a creature made in God's image and thus of infinite worth. And because of the eternal significance of human life, it's important to take seriously any involvement in preparing for, conceiving, anticipating, and raising children.

LET'S TALK ABOUT IT

1. Where did you get your ideas about family?
2. What seems right to you in terms of family size?
3. Do you feel pressure to produce children, if only from the future grandparents?
4. What about your calling as a child of God? How has God equipped you to serve? (For example, are you best equipped to disciple a large family or called to a zone of earth where a large family would be a stumbling block to the gospel?)
5. How financially secure do you think a couple must be before having children? Do you and your spouse agree on this?

CHAPTER 14

WHEN YOU'RE READY TO ADD TO YOUR FAMILY

Pre-conception Considerations

Many couples spend more time, thought, and energy on their weddings and honeymoons than on the marriages that will follow these events. They may even expend a lot of effort in finding the right car or the right home, but they put relatively little effort into thinking about the families they plan to have and, more specifically, about creating a prenatal environment that is conducive to the health of their children. In addition to understanding how the body works and the contraceptive methods available, couples should also be aware of some additional information. Pregnancy places enormous stress on the wife's body. The rising hormones and the growing infant affect virtually every body part, from a woman's toenails to her hair follicles. (Think of pregnancy as the Super Bowl of female bodily events.)

Every pregnant woman has a 3 to 4 percent baseline risk of giving birth to a baby with a birth defect and/or mental retardation.[1] And the risk of losing a pregnancy due to miscarriage ranges from one in three to one in two—quite a high number.[2] For this reason, women should take as many steps as possible to minimize problems.

Rarely does a mother's behavior actually contribute to pregnancy loss or birth defects, unless she is taking Accutane, using narcotics, or having an enormous number of X-rays. Yet it's reassuring to have done all the right things beforehand to avoid having regrets. Following is a suggested guide for preparation:

General fitness. Being physically fit contributes immeasurably to a successful pregnancy and increases the odds of a swift, full recovery after delivery. The woman wanting to conceive should strive to reach her ideal body weight and a reasonable level of cardiovascular fitness. Paying attention to diet, exercise, and rest are all significant parts of bodily preparation. Even a woman with a perfectly normal menstrual cycle can reduce some of the stress of pregnancy by establishing healthy habits.

Multivitamins. If your diet is well-balanced, multivitamins are probably unnecessary. But rare is the woman in our culture who can claim a well-balanced diet rich in all the necessary vitamins and minerals. Multiple studies have demonstrated that the risk of open spine defects (for example, spina bifida and anencephaly) is greatly reduced in women who take folic acid before conception. Folic acid can be taken in the form of a daily multivitamin. In a pre-conception visit, your physician can also prescribe vitamins with folic acid.

If you take herbal supplements, check with your doctor before continuing their use. While some remedies can help with pregnancy-related nausea, few have been tested for their effects during pregnancy, and the quality control on some products is totally lacking.

Rubella. Get a rubella titer, a test to determine whether you've had rubella (German measles). If needed, you can have a vaccination *before* attempting conception. Should pregnancy begin during a season in which rubella is spreading, the baby will be safeguarded by the mother's immunity. Rubella during pregnancy can have devastating effects on the developing infant.

Current medical problems. If you or your partner smoke, drink, or take illicit drugs, stop immediately. Also, the potential mother should avoid hot tubs or any situation that might cause overheating, especially in the first trimester. Discuss any history of STIs with your doctor, since some of these diseases could have an impact on pregnancy. A patient with AIDS or at high risk for HIV can be tested and advised appropriately. Many offices will also check for hepatitis, tuberculosis, anemia, or other blood disorders that might affect pregnancy. A patient with a family or personal history of hypertension, diabetes, or any chronic ailment needs to let the medical team know about the decision to attempt pregnancy so that good control can be achieved and any medications can be appropriately modified for the pregnant state.

Medications. Be sure your physician knows about all of the medications you are taking or have taken. Some drugs can be continued as normal, but pregnancy causes such diverse changes that many medications must be increased, switched, or monitored closely. Any history of allergies, particularly allergies to medications, should be noted by the doctor who will manage the pregnancy.

X-rays and dental work. If you need X-rays or dental work, try to have them done before conceiving. This is mostly for your own peace of mind. The normal levels of radiation a person is exposed to in most dental work and even chest and abdominal X-rays don't significantly increase the risk to the baby. The dentist can provide a lead shield for protection, and a radiologist can order X-rays that take a pregnancy into account. Nevertheless, mothers often feel anxiety about the risks associated with low-level radiation.

Contraceptives. If contraceptives have been altering your hormones, check with your doctor about how best to stop using them. You will probably need to switch to another form of contraceptive for at least one month before conceiving.

Genetic counseling. If you have a family history of inherited diseases, or if your ethnicity is a factor in genetic disease, consider getting genetic counseling. Arm yourselves with as many facts as possible. Check with your personal physician, who may refer you to a genetic counselor.

Pap smear. Every woman desiring to conceive should have regular Pap-smear screening. Your doctor can treat any cervical abnormalities before pregnancy begins, thus avoiding complications and risks.

Rh factor. Find out, by means of a simple blood test, if you are Rh negative. If you are negative and your husband is positive, you could later develop antibodies. With successive pregnancies, the situation worsens. It's easy to take steps to safeguard the pregnancy.

All of this may seem like a lot of testing, but every problem solved before conception is an enormous plus. While these precautions don't guarantee the desired pregnancy outcome, each can contribute to a greater likelihood of success.

Once a couple is ready to proceed in building their family, they can determine fertile days using the same methods discussed in our chapter on natural family planning. Most couples will conceive in three to six months. One in six couples, however, will find that they have a fertility problem.

When It Doesn't Work: Infertility

While most students in health class hear about preventing pregnancy, few hear about the one in six couples who will have difficulty conceiving. Infertility is often the first genuine crisis young couples of childbearing age experience together.

Research suggests that a woman's fertility begins to decline in her late twenties, whereas for the man, the decline happens later, in his thirties. This does not mean these years mark the end of fertility. Rather, problems tend to increase with delays.

> *There are three things that are never satisfied,*
>   *four that never say, "Enough!":*
> *the grave, the barren womb,*
>   *land, which is never satisfied with water,*
>   *and fire, which never says, "Enough!"*
>   *—Proverbs 30:15–16*

Apparently, it's like a natural law: the "barren womb" is never satisfied. And a common cause of infertility is delayed childbearing, something to keep in mind when considering contraception.

Infertility makes me feel like my pain is as bottomless as the Grand Canyon, my barrenness like Death Valley. I want to hide with my head under the covers.

I avoid people, especially the mall—especially at Christmas! I've pulled back in friendships with pregnant women and moms.

I have trouble concentrating at work. I feel guilty that my medical stuff is keeping my wife from being what she's always dreamed— a mommy.

Most fertile couples trying to conceive require three to six months before conception occurs. Infertility is defined as the failure to conceive and carry a pregnancy to term after one year of unprotected intercourse. So when is it time to seek help? If the wife is under thirty years old, is cycling regularly, and the husband has no difficulty with erection or ejaculation, attempting conception for a year makes sense. If, however, the wife's cycle is unpredictable or the husband has known medical issues, it makes good sense to seek help before waiting that long. Some testing is simple and reveals easily treatable issues. Approximately 60 percent of couples who seek medical help for fertility problems will go on to experience live birth.[3] Though we may make decisions about family building, ultimately love, marriage, fertility, and childbearing are in God's sovereign hands.

Adoption

Some couples desiring to build their families find they face insurmountable genetic issues or infertility. Or perhaps they sense a calling to parent children who otherwise would not have parents. For these couples, adoption may provide an answer.

Adoption has ancient and dignified origins. In the Bible, we see Moses and Esther, both members of the faith Hall of Fame, being raised by adoptive parents—Moses by Pharaoh's daughter and Esther by her cousin. The apostle Paul uses adoption as a metaphor for the believer's relationship with God as our Father once we are rightly related to him through his Son (Rom. 8:23; Gal. 4:5; Eph. 1:5). For those who desire to nurture the next generation, adoption is both a lovely reality and a fitting picture of how spiritual bonds can be stronger than blood.

Many excellent resources are available about adoption, and couples considering adoption should avail themselves of these helps. We will include here only a brief explanation with some key terms and factors to consider when seeking to adopt.

Legally, there are two kinds of adoption—*agency* adoption and *independent* (nonagency or private) adoption. In an agency adoption, the birth parents turn over their parental rights to the agency. In an independent adoption, the birth parents give consent directly to the adoptive parents.[4]

State laws control the adoption process, with four states allowing only agency adoption—Colorado, Connecticut, Delaware, and Massachusetts. More newborns are placed each year through independent adoptions than through agency adoptions because more birth parents pursue this option.[5] In fact, some twenty-five thousand to forty thousand infants are adopted annually through private adoption in the United States. These numbers exclude foster and relative adoptions, in which the adoptive parents tend to be well acquainted with the birth family's situation.[6]

Adoptive children come from two possible places—within the country (*domestic* adoption) and from other countries (*international* adoption). The number of international adoptions has been going up since the end of World War II. Currently, international adoptions represent about 10 percent of all U.S. adoptions. In the past ten years, increasing numbers of these children have come from the former Soviet Union and China.[7]

> *We've never been at the same place. I wanted treatment and my wife wanted adoption. Then last spring, I wanted to pursue treatment and she didn't think so.*

Couples have a variety of reasons for wanting to adopt. Perhaps they have been through lengthy battles with infertility. Others may see the number of parents killed by AIDS and sense God's leading to care for the remaining orphans. Some couples may have two boys and want to guarantee that the next one will be a girl. The reasons may be as varied as the couples seeking to add to their family size through adoption.

Because adoption is sometimes beset with misconceptions, we'll try to debunk a few here.

Myth: Couples must wait more than five years to get a child.

Fact: The average wait is actually less than two years.

Myth: Adoption is expensive.

Fact: We agree that adoption should be more affordable. Most couples pay around fifteen thousand dollars. The current U.S. ten-thousand-dollar tax credit helps.

Myth: Birth parents call all the shots, so they will reject us unless we agree to "shared parenting."

Fact: The law says adopting families determine the degree of openness. Many experts claim that open adoption—an arrangement in which the birth parent and the child have contact of some sort—is the best option. Others point out that little documented evidence exists to support either identified (open) or nonidentified (closed) arrangements. Yet even in identified adoption arrangements, the adopting family and birth families may never even meet. Involvement may be as limited as an occasional photo sent through a third party.

Myth: A lot of couples suffer having a child ripped out of their homes after placement.

Fact: While this is a truly traumatic experience, it happens in only 1 to 2 percent of all adoptions.

Myth: Adopted kids have more problems than biological kids do.

Fact: Research shows that adopted children turn out just as well as those raised by their biological parents.

Myth: Parents who adopt will never love their kids as much as if they had a genetic connection.

Fact: The very institution of marriage demonstrates that you can love as family a person to whom you are not genetically related.

Parents who have both biological and adopted children report that their ties to their adopted children are as strong as their ties to their genetic children.

Myth: Infertile couples should be the ones to adopt special-needs children and AIDS orphans. In terms of pure economics of supply and demand, these couples want kids and the kids need homes.

Fact: All of God's children are special creations. But just because special-needs children are available and they need parents doesn't mean a particular infertile couple must parent them. Sometimes those with some security in their parenting practices may be better suited to deal with the demands of a child with special needs. Both infertile and fertile couples who are considering adopting special-needs children must ask themselves, "Is this the best use of our resources—whether giftedness, financial, temperaments, or support systems?" Some couples are drawn to the unique challenges of raising a child with special needs; others are not. Those who sense no joy or peace at the prospect should feel no obligation to do so. For others, it is a noble, wonderful pursuit.

About half the number of birth parents who consider adoption change their minds before a baby is born and decide against placement. This risk can be decreased—though not eliminated—by working with reputable professionals who provide counseling both to birth parents and to the adopting families. An additional benefit of working with adoption professionals is that they can guide couples in knowing how to communicate the adoption experience to their children, their families, and their friends.

While adoption doesn't fulfill the infertile couple's desire to experience pregnancy, nor does it satisfy the longing to create a child together, it does fulfill the desire to nurture and parent the next generation. For these and other couples, adoption can be a wonderful way to build a family and a unique human picture of the divine relationship we have with our heavenly Father.

LET'S TALK ABOUT IT

1. At what ages would you and your spouse like to start your family? Is this realistic for you?
2. If you have chosen to delay having children (or more children), why? Are you in agreement on this?
3. Do you need to take steps to help secure a safer prenatal environment for your future child(ren)? If so, what would those steps be?
4. What concerns do you have about waiting to start a family?
5. Do you have any reason to believe infertility will be an issue for either of you?
6. What are your thoughts on adoption?
7. How do you feel about adopting a child with special needs? Foster parenting?

COMMUNICATION

FOR COUPLES
CONSIDERING CONCEPTION

By wisdom a house is built,
and by understanding it is established;
and by knowledge the rooms are filled
with all precious and pleasant riches.
—Proverbs 24:3–4 NASB

What do you believe about contraception? As the proverb above tells us, we build our homes by wisdom and understanding. Today one of the foundational elements of "building a house" is studying, discussing, and making some decisions about family building, expanding, and spacing. Following are questions for couples to consider together.

Family Background and Perspective

1. Describe your family, going back to your grandparents and including all siblings. Would you say you grew up in a large, a medium, or a small family?
2. Describe the division of labor in your home. Was a mother present? If so, did she stay home or work outside the home, or both? Examine the dynamics in your family of origin

regarding size and roles. Do you want your own home to be similar or different? How?

3. Think back to when you were fifteen. How did you envision your future family in terms of size and perhaps even the sex of your children? How did you envision your future? Did you envision having a vocation or being a stay-at-home spouse? What role did you see your future spouse playing in family life?

4. When you think about the primary purpose of sexual intimacy, would you say you see it as procreation, communication, recreation, spiritual transformation, or a combination of these?

5. Describe what you think it means for husband and wife to have a "one-flesh" relationship.

6. In your view, what are some biblical principles that are foundational to family building?

7. Describe your view of parental roles: Completely shared? One parent as primary nurturer? One parent as primary disciplinarian?

8. If you are already married, what decisions did you make prior to marriage about family planning?

9. Growing up, what were your beliefs about contraception? How were these beliefs formed?

10. What are your current thoughts about the ethics and morality of contraception, and how did you come to your current conclusions?

11. What do you believe is God's purpose for the family?

12. How do worship, stewardship, raising a godly generation, and personal prosperity fit into your vision for your family?

13. Take time to pray as a couple about family building. If you feel uncomfortable praying aloud together, join hands and silently thank God for your spouse. Then ask for wisdom in making these decisions together.

If Contraception Is an Option for You

1. Whose responsibility is contraception? Hers? His? Shared?

2. Are you comfortable using "artificial," external contraceptive methods such as hormonal adjustments?

3. Do you prefer methods of contraception that rely on physiology? Are you comfortable with the process of checking for

cervical mucus, temperature charting, and planned periodic abstinence?

4. How do you think physiological contraceptive approaches fit with the purpose of sexuality and the underlying theology?

5. Describe your sexual health and that of your spouse. Is intimacy a uniting, strong, delightful experience? Or is it more of a chore? How will the various methods of contraception affect your intimate life?

6. Consider each of the following contraceptive options as they relate to your own circumstances as a couple. Rate each from one to five by putting a check in the column, with five being positive and one being "no way." Then, for every method that ranked a three or higher, list the pros and cons for you and your spouse.

	1	2	3	4	5
a. Withdrawal					
b. Douching					
c. Breastfeeding					
d. Planned periodic abstinence					
e. Spermicides					
f. Male condom					
g. Female condom					
h. Cervical cap					
i. Diaphragm					
j. Combination oral contraceptives (COCs)					
k. Progesterone-only oral contraceptives (POPs)					
l. Implants or injections					
m. IUD					
n. Sponge					
o. Sterilization for him					
p. Sterilization for her					

7. How many children do you want?
8. How many children does your spouse want? Did you know this before you married? Have either of you changed your minds since you married?
9. Have you come to a consensus about family building? If not, what needs to happen for you to find a place of oneness?
10. In general, how do you as a couple handle conflict resolution? Would you say you "find one another's heart"? Does one of you tend to give in while the other gets his or her way? Do you both seek unity and godliness through love? If not, what steps need to be taken to move in that direction?
11. How do you feel about the spacing of children?
12. When and if you feel your family size is complete, what then? How do you plan to prevent pregnancy? Specify.
13. Do you have any reason to suspect that either of you might have a fertility problem?
14. After weighing the pros and cons, which method of contraception currently seems best in your circumstances?

According to the *Guinness Book of World Records*, a peasant from Moscow gave birth to sixty-nine children—including sixteen sets of twins, seven sets of triplets, and four sets of quadruplets. So even what we might consider a large family is not exactly record-setting. Still, using no contraception greatly increases a couple's chances that they'll have a family that's large by North American standards. A typical couple has about an 85 percent chance of conceiving each year during their childbearing years if they pay no attention to the wife's monthly cycle and enjoy a vigorous, contraceptive-free love life. What do you think of the prospect of having about fifteen children? How important is it to you to have a love life that's free of contraceptive concerns?

CHRISTIAN MEDICAL AND DENTAL ASSOCIATIONS POSITION STATEMENTS

1. Christian Medical and Dental Associations Statement on Possible Postfertilization Effects of Hormonal Birth Control

CMDA holds firmly that God is the Creator of life, that life begins at fertilization, and that all human life is of infinite value. We support measures to protect life from its earliest beginnings. CMDA recognizes that there are differing viewpoints among Christians regarding the broad issue of birth control and the use of contraceptives. The issue at hand, however, is whether hormonal birth control methods have postfertilization effects (i.e., cause abortion). CMDA has consulted many experts in the field of reproduction who have reviewed the scientific literature. While there are data that cause concern, our current scientific knowledge does not establish a definitive causal link between the routine use of hormonal birth control and abortion. However, neither are there data to deny a postfertilization effect.

Because this issue cannot be resolved with our current understanding, CMDA calls upon researchers to further investigate the mechanisms of action of hormonal birth control. Additionally, because the possibility of abortive effects cannot be ruled out, prescribers of hormonal birth control should consider informing patients of this potential factor.

We recognize the difficulties of providing informed consent while handicapped by lack of definitive information. However, counseling of patients may simply involve asking if they have concerns about potential postfertilization effects of these methods of birth control. In cases where concern exists, an explanation may follow that includes the known mechanisms of action (e.g., inhibition of ovulation and decreased sperm penetration), as well as the concern about the unanswered question of whether hormones negatively affect the very early stages of life.

CMDA respects and defends the right of our colleagues to refuse to prescribe hormonal birth control when they do so with the concern of a postfertilization effect.

We recognize that scientific reasoning is not the only factor that influences opinions about the use of hormonal birth control. But, while additional investigation is needed, current knowledge does not confirm or refute conclusions that routine use of hormonal birth control causes abortion. CMDA will continue to monitor new developments.[1]

September 1998

2. Christian Medical and Dental Associations Statement on Human Sexuality

God created human beings with many dimensions, one of which is their unique sexual nature. As men and women, we are physical, intellectual, emotional, relational, and spiritual beings, and thus distinguished from the rest of creation.

Many levels of sexual expression are possible between men and women.

One important expression of sexuality is friendship; the sexual differences between men and women enhance meaningful, warm, and healthy relationships. A second important area of sexual expression is intimacy between husband and wife. God has designed the most intimate expressions of sexuality, including intercourse, specifically for the marriage relationship. The Bible describes the covenantal relationship of love that God has for His people; the husband-wife relationship is analogous. Since God holds the marriage relationship close to His heart, its violation is a serious offense to Him.

Our integrated nature means that intimate sexual expression profoundly affects all dimensions of our being. While sexual expression outside of God's design may provide temporary pleasure, God's guidelines are meant to protect us from disease, fear, exploitation, and ultimately dehumanization.

CMDA affirms the biblical principles stated above. The following statements clarify these principles further:

1. Sexual intercourse is to be reserved exclusively for heterosexual marriage.
2. Single men and women who engage in sexual intercourse are outside of God's limits and are practicing sin.
3. Married people who have intercourse with anyone other than their marriage partner are defiling a marriage union which God has sealed and are in sin.
4. Like single heterosexuals who engage in heterosexual sex, or married persons who engage in extra-marital sex, homosexuals who engage in homosexual acts are practicing sin.
5. We condemn the perversion of sexuality in pornography, rape, incest, and all other forms of sexuality that deviate from the biblical norm for Christian marriage.
6. Family life teaching and sexual education are God-given responsibilities of parents. The Church's task is to assist both parents and youth in understanding their sexuality in the context of biblical values. When appropriate, sexual education should include risk behavior information and instruction on protective techniques to inhibit the spread of AIDS and all other sexually transmitted infections.
7. Education and protective techniques alone, however, will not stop the spread of AIDS. Our society needs to understand and acknowledge that there are compelling emotional, philosophical, medical, sociological, and historical reasons for practicing abstinence before marriage and fidelity within marriage.*

CMDA calls our world to affirm these biblical sexual morals. We recognize and acknowledge that many persons struggle with sexual temptation and sin, and that all of us have fallen short of God's standards. We testify that God is just, merciful, loving, and faithful, and that He will, if we ask Him, forgive us of our sins and bring us into an intimate relationship with Him.

*From the CMDA Statement on AIDS
Approved by the CMDA House of Delegates
Passed unanimously May 3, 1990
Toronto, Canada

3. Christian Medical and Dental Associations Statement on Abortion

1. We oppose the practice of abortion and urge the active development and employment of alternatives.
2. The practice of abortion is contrary to:

    *   The revealed, written Word of God.
    *   Respect for the sanctity of human life.
    *   Traditional, historical, and Judeo-Christian medical ethics.

3. We believe that biblical Christianity affirms certain basic principles which dictate against interruption of human gestation; namely:

    *   The ultimate sovereignty of a loving God, the Creator of all life.
    *   The great value of human life transcending that of the quality of life.
    *   The moral responsibility of human sexuality.

4. While we recognize the right of physicians and patients to follow the dictates of individual conscience before God, we affirm the final authority of Scripture, which teaches the sanctity of human life.

Approved by the CMDA House of Delegates
Passed with a vote of 59 for, 3 opposed, 1 abstention
May 4, 1985
San Diego, California

4. Christian Medical and Dental Associations Statement on Reproductive Technology

The family is the basic social unit as designed by God. It is formed as a man and woman make an exclusive marital commitment for love, companionship, intimacy, and spiritual union. As a result of their physical union, children may be added to the family.

Children are a gift and responsibility from God to the family. Parents are entrusted with providing and modeling love, nurture, protection, and spiritual training. The inability to have children need not diminish the fullness of the family.

Infertile couples may choose adoption or seek medical care when they desire children. Adoption emulates God's adoption of us as spiritual children. Some reproductive technologies are an appropriate exercise of mankind's God-given creativity.

Certain reproductive technologies may present direct and indirect dangers to the family. As technology permits further divergence from normal physiologic reproduction, it increasingly leads to perplexing moral dilemmas. Not every technological procedure may be morally justified.

The principles which can guide the development and implementation of reproductive technologies include the following: First, conception resulting from the union of a wife's egg and her husband's sperm is the biblical design. Second, individual human life begins at fertilization; therefore, God intends for us to protect it. Third, God holds us morally responsible for our genetic offspring.

Statement

CMDA approves the following procedures as consistent with God's design for the family:

- Education about fertilization
- Medical treatment (e.g., ovulation-inducing drugs)
- Surgical intervention (e.g., for anatomic abnormalities hindering fertility)
- Artificial insemination by husband (AIH)
- Adoption
- In vitro fertilization (IVF) with husband's sperm and wife's egg, with subsequent:

  a. Transfer to uterus (ER-embryo replacement)
  b. Zygote intrafallopian transfer (ZIFT)

- Gamete intrafallopian transfer (GIFT)—husband's sperm and wife's egg
- Cryopreservation of sperm or egg

CMDA cannot speak with certainty about the place of the following procedures in God's design for the family:

- Artificial insemination by donor (AID)
- In vitro fertilization (donor egg or donor sperm)
- Gamete intrafallopian transfer (donor egg or donor sperm)
- Zygote intrafallopian transfer (donor egg or donor sperm)

    Reason: While there is no clear biblical support for the concept of the introduction of a third party, there is strong biblical support for the ideal of a family as defined in the preamble of this statement.

- Cryopreservation of embryos with specific safeguards

    Reason: Cryopreservation raises the possibility of embryo destruction and preservation of excessive embryos.

CMDA opposes the following procedures as inconsistent with God's design for the family:

- Selective abortion for embryo reduction or sex selection
- Surrogate mother procedures
- Transfer of excessive numbers of embryos to a recipient mother
- Uterine lavage for embryo transfer
- Discarding of embryos
- Non-therapeutic experimentation with embryos

Conclusion

CMDA affirms the need for continued moral scrutiny of our developing reproductive technology as it impacts the family. We recognize that as physicians we must use our creative capacity within the limits of God's design. Couples who suffer from infertility should be encouraged to seek pastoral guidance and counsel, as well as to pray for God's wisdom in the use of these technologies.

Addendum

In this statement, embryo refers to the conceptus from the moment of fertilization. We do not differentiate between the new term "pre-embryo" and embryo.

Guidelines for Cryopreservation of Embryos

1. Cryopreservation of embryos should be done with the sole intent of future transfer to the genetic mother.
2. Embryos should be produced from the husband's sperm and the wife's eggs.
3. A limited number of embryos should be produced to eliminate cryopreservation of excessive numbers of embryos.
4. There should be pre-agreement on the part of the couple that if the wife becomes pregnant, all remaining frozen embryos will be transferred back into her at future times of her choice.
5. There should also be pre-agreement that in a situation in which the embryos cannot be transferred to the wife (e.g., where the wife dies or has a hysterectomy), they will be adopted by another couple who desire to have a child for themselves by having the embryos transferred to the adoptive mother.

Approved by the CMDA House of Delegates
Passed with a vote of 63 for, 1 opposed
May 3, 1990
Toronto, Canada

NOTES

Preface

1. Despite the fact that we have edited this work accordingly, we encourage readers to avoid making the assumption that those in other contexts who use the terms *birth control* and *family planning* embrace an ungodly worldview. These terms are often used as being synonymous with *contraception* in our culture, even by those within orthodox Christianity. Some who insist that the term *family planning* is a secular humanist's euphemism for abortion still refer to "natural *family planning*" as a means of timing and spacing one's children.
2. From the FamilyLife Manifesto. The entire manifesto is available at www.familylife.com.

Chapter 2: You Won't Get Pregnant If ...

1. Kathleen London, "History of Birth Control," Yale New Haven Teachers Institute, http://www.yale.edu/ynhti/curriculum/units/1982/6/82.06.03.x.html (accessed March 27, 2004).
2. Norman E. Himes, *Medical History of Contraception* (New York: Gamut, 1963); Linda Gordon, *Woman's Body, Woman's Right: A Social History of Birth Control in America* (New York: Penguin, 1976); London, "The History of Birth Control."
3. Jo Ann Rosenfeld and Kevin Everett, "Lifetime Patterns of Contraception and Their Relationship to Unintended Pregnancies," *Journal of Family Practice* (September 2000): www.jfponline.com/jfp_toc.asp?year=5&month=9.

Chapter 3: The Why of Sex

1. We see the combination of these same words, "desire" and "rule," used one chapter later to show a power struggle (Gen. 4:7 KJV).
2. Current reproductive technologies, including cloning research, are exceptions to this axiom. Nevertheless, the ideal since the time of Eden has been that the one-flesh relationship between a man and woman in a committed, monogamous relationship is the context in which human reproduction happens.

3. Al Mohler, "Can Christians Use Birth Control?" Crosswalk.com, http://www.crosswalk.com/news/weblogs/mohler/ (accessed March 30, 2004).
4. Gavin de Becker, *Protecting the Gift* (New York: Dell, 1999), cited in Meryn G. Callander, "Myth: Naming Genitals with Euphemisms Is Appropriate and Harmless to Children," Wellness Associates website, www.thewellspring.com/TWO/23genital_euphemisms.html, ©2000.

Chapter 4: How Our Bodies Work

1. Dopamine and apomorphine.
2. Notably serotonin, which is increased by selective serotonin reuptake inhibitors (SSRIs) such as Prozac, Paxil, and Zoloft.
3. Other releasers of this marvelous chemical family include chili peppers, hearty laughter, and chocolate, though not necessarily all at the same time.
4. While medications, surgery, and other high-tech procedures are available to assist those who are anatomically unable to reproduce, this book will focus on the uncomplicated situation.
5. Richard Lacayo, "Are You Man Enough?" *Time*, April 24, 2000, 58.
6. Glenn Elbert, "Speed of a Sperm Cell," *The Physics Factbook*, http://hypertextbook.com/facts/2000/EugeneKogan.shtml.
7. A. Bahat et al., "Thermotaxis of Mammalian Sperm Cells: A Potential Navigation Mechanism in the Female Genital Tract," *Nature Medicine* 9 (January 2003): 149–50.
8. For a more thorough exploration of this subject, consult Robert Pyne, *Humanity and Sin: The Creation, Fall and Redemption of Humanity* (Nashville: Word, 1999). Of particular interest is chapter 5: "The Immaterial Aspect of Human Nature."
9. Because the events surrounding fertilization happen in such rapid succession, it's fine to say that life begins at fertilization. To be technically correct, however, we specify life as beginning when DNA is activated, or syngamy. In cloning, there is no "moment of fertilization," yet there is the beginning of human life when chromosomes are activated by chemical or electrical stimulation.

Chapter 5: Planned Periodic Abstinence

1. A similar product is the Donna (www.thedonna.com), but it is currently not sold as a contraceptive device in the United States.
2. Elizabeth Pritchett, "Ovulation Method of Natural Family Planning: The Creighton Model-NaProEducation System," The Human Sexuality Web, http://www.umkc.edu/sites/hsw/health/birthcontrol/index2html (accessed March 6, 2004).
3. Theresa Notare, "Celebrate Natural Family Planning," *Denver Catholic Register*, July 17, 2002.

4. Allen J. Wilcox et al., "Time of Implantation of the Conceptus and Loss of Pregnancy," *New England Journal of Medicine* 340, no. 23 (June 10, 1999): 1796–99. The researchers speculated that embryos that implant more slowly may be imperfect in some way. This report is based on the careful testing of daily urine samples from about two hundred women from North Carolina. This relatively large study involving normal, fertile women confirms the more tentative data from two small reports put out in 1991 and 1993.

Chapter 6: A Trip to the Pharmacy

1. Nicholas Kristof, "The Secret War on Condoms," *New York Times,* January 10, 2003.
2. "Effectiveness of Male Latex Condoms in Protecting against Pregnancy and Sexually Transmitted Infections," World Health Organization Fact Sheet no. 243, (June 2000), http://www.who.int/ mediacentre/factsheets/fs243/en/ (accessed March 26, 2004).
3. "Barrier Contraceptives: A Growing Array of Options," Health Square, http://www.healthsquare.com. This site has a variety of helpful diagrams.
4. Norman Hinds, *Medical History of Contraception*, cited in "Lemons and AIDS," AIDS Information Services website, amended March 2004, www.aids.net.au/lemons-history.htm. More recently, Roger Short, M.D., from the Department of Obstetrics and Gynecology at the University of Melbourne, who also runs a lab at the Royal Women's Hospital, checked the efficacy of the lemon. He and his associates found that a 20 percent concentration of lemon juice in fresh human ejaculate irreversibly immobilized 100 percent of spermatozoa in less than thirty seconds. They also found that a 10 percent concentration of lemon juice was enough to quickly kill HIV. See Roger Short, "Get Those Juices Flowing," *The Australian*, December 21, 2002.
5. Kate Zernike, "Many Women Gleeful at Old Friend's Encore," *New York Times*, March 7, 2003.
6. Mayo Clinic, "Contraceptive Sponge: The Right Form of Birth Control for You?" CNN.com, http://www.cnn.com/HEALTH/library/WO/00045.html (accessed March 27, 2004).
7. Cervical Cap Ltd., http://www.cervcap.com/about.html (accessed March 27, 2004).

Chapter 7: What about the Pill?

1. For example, the first week of pills may have 0.5 mg of progesterone and 35 mcg of estradiol; the second week, 0.75 mg progesterone, 35 mcg estradiol; the third week, 1mg of progesterone, 35 mcg of estradiol. So each pill within the set of seven in the triphasic pills has the same combination of hormone, but the set differs from the compound

contained in sets for the other weeks. The total amount of progesterone ingested in a complete cycle is less than that contained in the monophasic pill pack, which would have 1 mg of progesterone and 35 mcg of estrogen in each pill (21 pills at 1 mg = 21 mg of progesterone per month). The triphasic pack would have 7 pills at 0.5 mg, then 7 pills at .75 mg, and finally 7 at 1 mg., so ultimately the patient receives substantially less progesterone than with monophasic pills. Few pills alter the estrogen levels.

2. Laura Berman, quoted in "You've Come a Long Way: Which New Birth Control Choices Would Work for You?" *ABC News*, September 25, 2003, http://abcnews.go.com/sections/GMA/HealthyWoman/GMA030925Birth_control_choices.html (accessed March 10, 2004).

3. Ortho-McNeil Pharmaceutical Company, "Women Prefer the Patch: In One Year Ortho Evra Becomes the Fastest Growing Hormonal Contraceptive on the Market," July 25, 2003, http://www.ortho-mcneil.com/news/article072503.html. The survey was conducted in November 2001.

4. Nathalie Bajos et al., "Contraception: from Accessibility to Efficiency," *Human Reproduction* 18, no. 5 (May 2003): 994–99.

5. There is some concern about the noncontraceptive use of combination pills to treat menopausal symptoms. A Women's Health Initiative (WHI) study found that certain combination pills used for this purpose may increase the risk of breast cancer by 24 percent. The pills may also make breast cancer grow more rapidly and behave more aggressively. In addition, the WHI study found that the combination pill increased the risk of stroke by 41 percent and the risk of heart attack by 26 percent, even when such factors as smoking, diabetes, and high blood pressure were taken into account. Researchers speculate that the progesterone in the combination pill is responsible for these effects. Because the WHI study involved postmenopausal women, it is unclear whether the same adverse effects occur in younger women using combination pills for contraception. Additional studies are needed to clarify the answer to this question.

6. S. O. Skouby and K. R. Petersen, "Clinical Experience with the Recently Developed Progestogens," *International Journal of Fertility* 36, suppl. no. 1 (1991): 32–37.

7. J. Drife, "Benefits and Risks of Oral Contraceptives," *Advanced Contraception,* suppl. no. 6, (December 1990): 15–25.

8. C. Caruso et al., "A Prospective Study Evidencing Rhinomanometric and Olfactometric Outcomes in Women Taking Oral Contraceptives," *Human Reproduction* 16, no. 1 (November 2001): 2288–94. This study involved sixty women, ages eighteen to forty, who were not taking the pill. The researchers tested the women's ability to detect six distinctive substances at three defined times in the menstrual cycle. The women's sense of

smell was most sensitive around the time of ovulation. The volunteers were then prescribed oral contraceptives. After three months' use, their sensitivity to smell was retested and no change was noted.

9. Women who carry a certain cancer-prone gene mutation and who took oral contraceptives at a young age or before 1975 face an increased risk of developing breast cancer. The study that supports this finding involved more than 2,600 women in eleven countries. Formulations of the pill are different today from what they were prior to 1975, when they contained more estrogen. See S. Narod et al., "Oral Contraceptives and the Risk of Breast Cancer in BRCA1 and BRCA2 Mutation Carriers," *Journal of the National Cancer Institute* 94, (December 2002): 1773–79.

Chapter 8: Do Birth Control Pills Cause Abortion?

1. J. L. Schwartz et al., "Predicting Risk of Ovulation in New Start Oral Contraceptive Users," *Obstetrics and Gynecology* 99, no. 2 (February 2002): 177–82.

2. Ibid

3. K. Elomaa, "Omitting the First Oral Contraceptive Pills of the Cycle Does Not Automatically Lead to Ovulation," *American Journal of Obstetrics and Gynecology* 179, no. 1, (July 1998): 41–46.

4. P. Rosenbaum, "Inhibition of Ovulation by a Novel Progestogen (Drospirenone) Alone or in Combination with Ethinylestradiol," *European Journal of Contraception and Reproductive Health Care* 5, no. 1 (March 2000): 16–24.

5. W. G. Rossmanith, "A Comparative Randomized Trial on the Impact of Two Low-Dose Oral Contraceptives on Ovarian Activity, Cervical Permeability, and Endometrial Receptivity," *Contraception* 56, no. 1 (July 1997): 23–30.

6. C. Fitzgerald et al., "A Comparison of the Effects of Two Monophasic Low Dose Oral Contraceptives on the Inhibition of Ovulation," *Advanced Contraception* 10, no. 1 (March 1994): 5–18.

7. J. Spona, "Inhibition of Ovulation by an Oral Contraceptive Containing 100 Micrograms Levonorgestrel in Combination with 20 Micrograms Ethinylestradiol," *Contraception* 54, no. 2 (November 1996): 299–304.

8. In the November 2004 issue of *Fertility and Sterility*, researchers citing their findings in separate articles conclude that one cannot determine receptivity of the endometrium to a pregnancy even using a microscope on biopsied tissue. Thus the idea that the rather inaccurate measurements of the thickness and thinness of the uterine lining achieved by endometrial biopsy or ultrasound may not be a significant factor in the possibility of abortifacient effect. In summary, the key finding is that "maturation stage of the endometrium is not critical for pre-

dicting successful pregnancy." See especially P. G. McDonough *et al*, "Grading a Developmental Continuum—Elegy on the Rise and Fall of the Endometrial Biopsy," *Fertility and Sterility* 82, no. 5 (November 2004): 1286–92.

Chapter 9: Other Hormone Therapy Options

1. "Lunelle: Monthly Birth Control Shot," University of Chicago, http://scc.uchicago.edu/lunelle.htm (accessed March 26, 2004).
2. "Patient Information about Lunelle," Pfizer, http://www.pfizer.com, and "Lunelle Monthly Injection," Women's Health Information, http://www.fwhc.org/birth-control/lunelle.htm.
3. Anne Marie Chaker, *Wall Street Journal*, August 1, 2003.
4. Carol Buia, "Drugstore: Birth Controls," *Time*, August 5, 2002, www.time.com/time/archive.html.
5. L. S. Abrams et al., "Pharmacokinetics of Norelgestromin and Ethinyl Estradiol Delivered by a Contraceptive Patch (Ortho Evra/Evra) under Conditions of Heat, Humidity, and Exercise," *Journal of Clinical Pharmacology* 41 (December 2001): 1301–9.
6. "What Is NuvaRing?" NuvaRing, http://www.nuvaring.com/Consumer/howDoIStart/index.asp, (accessed January 20, 2004).
7. Chris Kahleborn et al., "Postfertilization Effect of Hormonal Emergency Contraception," *Annals of Pharmacotherapy* 36, no. 3 (March 2002): 465–70. The available evidence for a postfertilization effect is moderately strong, whether hormonal emergency contraception is used in the preovulatory, ovulatory, or postovulatory phase of the menstrual cycle.
8. "Now Mbeki Probes Contraceptive Drug," ANC (African National Conference) *Daily News Briefing*, April 19, 2000.
9. "How Depo-Provera Works," Depo-Provera, http://www.depoprovera.com.
10. Herndon, Emily and Miriam Zieman, "Mirena: New Contraceptive Options," *American Family Physician* 4 (February 15, 2004): 853–64.

Chapter 10: Under the Knife

1. National Center for Health Statistics, "Surgical Sterilization in the United States: Prevalence and Characteristics: 1965–1995," June 1998, p. 1, http://www.cdc.gov/reproductivehealth/pdf/sr23_20.pdf (accessed January 27, 2004).
2. "Contraceptive Sterilization: Executive Summary," Engender Health, http://www.engenderhealth.org/res/offc/steril/factbook/execsum.html.
3. The information on laparoscopy is adapted from our book *The Infertility Companion: Hope and Help for Couples Facing Infertility* (Grand Rapids: Zondervan, 2004).

4. John F. Kerin et al., "Hysteroscopic Sterilization Using a Micro-Insert Device: Results of a Multicentre Phase II Study," *Human Reproduction* 18, no. 6 (June 2003): 1223–30.
5. "Female Sterilization: Essure," Reproductive Health Reproline Online, http://www.reproline.jhu.edu/english/1fp/1advances/1femster/essure.htm.
6. Mark D. Levie, "Sterilization 2002" (highlights from the thirty-first annual meeting of the American Association of Gynecologic Laparoscopists), *Medscape Ob/Gyn and Women's Health* 7, no. 2 (December 30, 2002), http://www.medscape.com/px/login (accessed January 27, 2004).
7. International Society for Gynecologic Endoscopy, "Hysteroscopic Sterilization with Essure," http://www.isge.orgl.
8. Allan Centre for Women, "Endometrial Ablation," http://www.allancentreforwomen.com/endometrial.html (accessed February 9, 2004).
9. V. L. Holt et al., "Oral Contraceptives, Tubal Sterilization, and Functional Ovarian Cyst Risk," *Obstetrics and Gynecology* 102, no. 2 (August 2003): 252–58.
10. National Center for Health Statistics, "Surgical Sterilization in the United States," 9.
11. "Deciding about Tubal Sterilization," *American Family Physician* 67, no. 6 (March 15, 2003), http://www.aafp.org/afp.

Chapter 11: His Turn

1. Jim McCartney, "Clip Provides Quicker, Cheaper, Less Painful Alternative to Vasectomy," *Kansas City Star,* April 30, 2003, http://www.kansascity.com/mld/kansascity/news/nation/5748123.htm?1c (accessed March 27, 2004).
2. "Frequently Asked Questions," Vasectomy Medical.com, September 21, 2003, http://www.vasectomymedical.com/vasectomy-questions.html#ques5 (accessed January 27, 2004).
3. McCartney, "Alternative to Vasectomy."
4. "Ask Your Question," Medhelp, http://www.medhelp.org/ forums/urology/archive/1182.html (accessed February 2, 2004).
5. "Deciding about Tubal Sterilization," *American Family Physician* 67, no. 6 (March 15, 2003), http://www.aafp.org/afp.
6. Maureen B. Gardner, "Facts about Vasectomy," Office of Research Reporting, National Institute of Child Health and Human Development (NICHD), Shenandoah Women's Health Care, http://www.swhc.net/Patient%20Education/vasectomy.htm.
7. Ibid.
8. Ibid.
9. "Fact Sheet: Vasectomy," Vasclip, http://www.vasclip.com, (accessed February 7, 2004).

Chapter 12: The Future of Contraception

1. Pliny, *Natural History*, cited in John R. Riddle, "Oral Contraceptives and Early-Term Abortifacients during Classical Antiquity and the Middle Ages," *Past and Present* no. 132 (August 1991): 3–32.
2. Rachel Newcome, "Male Pill on the Way?" British United Provident Association, October 13, 2003, http://www.bupa.co.uk/health_ information/html/health_news/131003malepill.html.
3. Juliet Lawrence Wilson, "A Seed of Doubt That is Just Too Deeply Implanted," Scotsman.com (*Evening News*, Scotland), March 2, 2004, http://news.scotsman.com/archive.cfm?id=244972004 (accessed March 29, 2004).
4. Advanced Legal Services, "Norplant Contraceptive Implants," October 2002, http://www.mindspring.com/~advance/norplant.htm.
5. "News and Events: Organon and Schering Start Large Clinical Trial to Test the 'Male Pill' in Fourteen European centers," Organon International press release, January 21, 2004.
6. Audrey Schulman, "The De-Sperm-inator," *Grist Magazine*, August 19, 2003, www.grist.org/news/maindish/2003/08/13/sperminator/.
7. Li Peng et al., "An Antimicrobial Peptide Gene Found in the Male Reproductive System of Rats," *Science* 29 (March 2, 2001): 1783–85, http://www.sciencemag.org. This story also appeared in "Male Contraceptive Could Fight STDs," British Broadcasting Corporation, March 1, 2001 http://news.bbc.co.uk/1/hi/sci/tech/1196643.stm.
8. "Male Contraceptive Trial Has 100 Percent Success," *New Scientist*, October 6, 2003, http://www.newscientist.com/news/news.jsp?id =ns99994237.
9. "Whatever Happened to the Male Contraceptive Pill?" *The Independent* (London), September 1, 2003.
10. Lohiya, Nirmal, et al., "Vas Deferens, a Site of Male Contraception: An Overview," *Asian Journal of Andrology* 3 (June 2001): 87–95.
11. Sreelatha Menon, "ICMR Takes a Shot at a Male Contraceptive," *Indian Express Newspapers*, October 25, 2002.
12. "Vasectomy and Vasovasectomy (Reversal Surgery)," *Health and Age*, August 31, 2003, http://www.healthandage.com.
13. Audrey Schulman, "The Sperminator: A New Injection for Men Could Shake Up the World of Contraceptives," *Grist Magazine*, August 13, 2003.
14. "Methods—Pharmaceuticals—Gossypol," Male Contraceptives, http://www.malecontraceptives.org/methods/gossypol_frame.html.
15. Ibid.
16. Ganapati Mudur, "News: India to Ban Female Sterilisation with Malaria Drug," *British Medical Journal* 316 (March 28, 1998): 955.
17. Ganapati Mudur, "News Extra: Use of Antibiotic in Contraceptive Trial Sparks Controversy," *British Medical Journal* 328 (January 24, 2004): 188.

18. P. A. Fail et al., "Comparative Effects of Quinacrine and Erythromycin in Adult Female Rats: A Nonsurgical Sterilization Study," *Fertility and Sterility* 73, no. 2 (February 2000): 387–94.

Chapter 13: Unless the Lord Builds the House ...

1. The economist mentioned was Kenneth E. Boulding.
2. Karen S. Peterson, "Study: Joint Custody Best for Kids after Divorce," *USA Today*, March 24, 2002. This article is also available at the American Responsible Divorce Network website, http://www.responsible-divorce.com/reform/apa-study.htm.
3. K. T. Magnuson, "Marriage, Procreation, and Infertility: Reflections on Genesis," *Southern Baptist Journal of Theology* 4, no. 1 (Spring 2000): 26–42.
4. R. A. Barclay, *The Law Givers* (New York: Abingdon, 1964), 39.
5. Daniel Block, Associate Dean of Scripture and Interpretation, the Southern Baptist Theological Seminary, "Old Testament Perspective on Marriage," (lecture, the Southern Baptist Theological Seminary, October 2001).
6. "Facts about Single People," American Association for Single People, http://www.unmarriedamerica.org/facts.html.
7. Laurie Evans et al., "Abortion Surveillance: 2000," *MMWR Surveillance Summaries* 52, (November 28, 2003): 1–32.
8. Ibid.
9. Ibid., chart 14.

Chapter 14: When You're Ready to Add to Your Family

1. Emory Genetics Laboratory, "General Population Risk for Birth Defects," http://www.emory.edu/WHSC/MED/GENETICS/pdf/Emory_Human_Genetics_General_Population_Risk_for_Birth_Defects.PDF (accessed March 27, 2004).
2. Some researchers even estimate that the pregnancy loss rate is as high at 75 percent. See Carolyn Coulam, "Recurrent Pregnancy Loss," *INCIID (International Council for Infertility Information Dissemination) Insights*, October 2002, http://www.inciid.org/newsletter/oct/coulam2.html (accessed February 16, 2004).
3. For an exhaustive treatment of this subject, consult our book *The Infertility Companion.*
4. For a fuller discussion of this subject, consult the *The Infertility Companion*, from which this is adapted.
5. Mark T. McDermott, "Overview of Independent or Private Adoption," http://www.theadoptionadvisor.com/independent.html.
6. Karen Spar, "Foster Care and Adoption Stats," Congressional Research Service (CRS) report prepared for the House Subcommittee on Human Resources, January 15, 1997. Available at Casanet.org (Court Appointed

Special Advocate), http://www.casanet.org/library/foster-care/fost
.htm.

7. In 1993, sixty-six countries, including the United States, agreed to ethical ground rules to prevent the abduction, trafficking, and sale of human beings. Their joint statement affirms that family and culture are a child's birthright and, whenever possible, children should remain with their biological families. The full statement from the 1993 Hague Convention on Protection of Children and Co-operation in Respect of Intercountry Adoption is available at http://www.hcch.net/e/conventions/text33e.html.

Appendix 2

1. This statement is available at http://www.cmds.org.

GLOSSARY

Ablation. See endometrial ablation and uterine ablation.

Abortifacient. An agent, such as a medication, that induces abortion, whether by intent or as a secondary effect.

Accutane. A brand-name medication used in the treatment of severe acne. If pregnancy occurs while taking Accutane in any amount, even for a short duration, there is an extremely high risk that a severely affected infant will be born. There is also an increased risk of miscarriage.

Adenomyosis. The presence of endometrial tissue within the myometrium, which is the muscular portion of the uterine wall.

Adhesion. Adjacent tissues sticking to one another. Adhesions are caused by infection, irritation, or inflammation. They can be thin and filmy like plastic wrap or thick, tenacious, and difficult to divide. Adhesions in the abdominal cavity, fallopian tubes, or inside the uterus can interfere with the egg's movement and the implantation of the embryo.

AIDS. Acquired immunodeficiency syndrome, caused by HIV (the human immunodeficiency virus).

Amenorrhea. The absence or abnormal cessation of menstruation.

Androgens. Hormones that cause masculine-type changes, such as oily skin, facial hair, and weight gain. When elevated, these hormones may lead to fertility problems in both men and women.

Anencephaly. A congenital absence of the major portion of the brain, skull, and scalp.

Antibodies. Proteins made by the body to fight or attack foreign substances entering the body. Antibodies normally prevent infection, but sometimes they attack gametes or embryos, causing infertility.

Antisperm antibodies. An immune system response to sperm, in which immune cells (the body's protective cells) attach themselves to sperm and inhibit their movement and ability to fertilize.

Blastocyst. An early stage of embryo development (reached approximately five days after fertilization). The blastocyst looks like a hollow ball of cells with a secondary cluster of cells on the inner wall at one end. The inner group of cells will develop into the baby, while the outer sphere becomes the supporting structures, including the placenta and amniotic sac.

Breakthrough ovulation. Ovulation that takes place despite hormonal manipulation aimed at preventing it. Also called escape ovulation.

Cervix. The lower portion of the uterus that extends into the vagina.

Cervical cap. A female barrier method of contraception in which a latex rubber, thimble-shaped device covers the entire roof of the vagina. Must be initially fitted by a physician.

Cervical mucus. A substance that plugs the opening of the cervix. Usually it prevents sperm and bacteria from entering the womb, but at ovulation, under the influence of estrogen, the mucus becomes thin, watery, and stretchy to allow sperm to pass.

Cervical os. The small opening in the middle of the cervix that allows the sperm in and the menses out. The cervical os opens slightly as the fertile window approaches.

Chromosome. The cell structure that carries the genes. Humans have forty-six chromosomes, half coming from the egg and half from the sperm. At fertilization, a human life has all the chromosomes it will ever have. Within the first twenty-four hours following egg penetration by the sperm, the chromosomes in the egg align with the chromosomes from the sperm, resulting in the creation of a unique human being with the full complement of forty-six chromosomes (syngamy). If this process succeeds, this new human, now only a one-cell being (zygote), begins to divide and thrive.

Cilia. Small hairlike projections that line the inside of the fallopian tubes. Their wavelike action facilitates the movement of the egg toward the uterus.

Clitoris. The sex organ of the female that has no other known function than to provide sexual pleasure. It contains an enormous number of sensory nerves and in terms of sexual sensation is the female counterpart to the head of the penis.

Cloning. The procedure in which an embryo is grown from a single somatic cell of its parent, making it genetically identical to that parent or gene donor.

COC. Combination oral contraceptive. COCs include a combination of hormones: estrogen and progestin, a synthetic progesterone.

Coitus interruptus. Also called the withdrawal method or onanism in some cultures. An unreliable method of contraception in which, during sexual intercourse, the man removes his penis from the woman's vagina just before his orgasm so that his semen is ejaculated outside of the vagina.

Conception. The event that takes place when the maternal DNA in the egg aligns with paternal DNA from the sperm and activates, resulting in the creation of a unique human being. (In normal human fertilization, this happens shortly after the sperm penetrates the egg.) Some texts define conception as the event we call "implantation," which is the point at which the dividing embryo, containing one hundred to two hundred cells, implants (attaches to the uterine wall). Implantation takes place nearly a week after conception. Some texts use *conception* and *implantation* as synonyms. For this reason, we avoid the term. In our view, conception and implantation are separate events, occurring approximately seven days apart.

Condom. A sheath worn over the penis that serves as a male barrier contraceptive device.

Contraception. The deliberate prevention of fertilization.

Contraceptive patch. A female contraceptive device that delivers hormones through the skin and into the bloodstream.

Cornua. The horns of the uterus. The place where the tubes enter the uterus.

Corpus luteum. Latin for "yellow body." The hormone-producing structure resulting from ovulation of a mature follicle. It is yellow in appearance and is essential for the normal production of progesterone. Progesterone causes the slight rise in basal temperature that happens at the midpoint of the menstrual cycle. If the corpus luteum does not function as it should, the uterine lining may fail to support a pregnancy. Once fertilization of the eggs occurs, the corpus luteum produces progesterone that maintains the uterine lining, supporting the implanted embryo. If the corpus luteum fails to produce progesterone for long enough or in sufficient quantities, the endometrium is unable to sustain a pregnancy. This is called a luteal phase defect (LPD).

Diaphragm. A female barrier method of contraception in which a round latex device, roughly the size of the palm of the hand, fits over the cervix. Must be initially fitted by a physician. Recommended for use in conjunction with a spermicide.

DNA (deoxyribonucleic acid). The molecular basis of heredity that makes up the genes, within the chromosomes that determine all of a person's physical characteristics.

Ectopic pregnancy. A potentially life-threatening situation in which pregnancy takes place outside of the uterus, usually in a fallopian tube.

Ejaculation. The sudden discharge of semen at the moment of male orgasm.

Embryo. A human life in its earliest stages. (After approximately twelve weeks of age, it is called a fetus.)

Emergency contraception. Also called the morning-after pill. A series of combination oral contraceptives taken in a way that initially spikes a woman's estrogen and progesterone levels. The patient then abruptly stops taking any pills, removing the hormonal support for the endometrium. If the pills are taken after ovulation, the morning-after pill works as an abortifacient.

Endometrial ablation. Also called uterine ablation. An outpatient surgical procedure to eliminate or reduce bleeding from the uterus by destroying the uterine lining through use of heated fluid, electrical cautery, or various types of laser.

Endometriosis. A condition in which endometrial tissue forms outside the uterus, sometimes causing pain and infertility.

Endometrium. The lining of the uterus, which grows and sheds in response to hormonal stimulation; the tissue designed to nourish the implanted embryo.

Endorphins. Natural narcotics manufactured in the brain to reduce sensitivity to pain and stress. The body produces endorphins in response to orgasm, exercise, laughter, chocolate, and chili peppers.

Epididymis. A system of ducts from the testis that contain and transport sperm.

Erection. The process during which the penis becomes engorged with blood, causing it to swell and become rigid.

Erythromycin. A common antibiotic. It causes scar tissue when placed at the upper part of the uterine cavity, so it is being researched for use as a means of permanent female sterilization.

Escape ovulation. Ovulation that takes place despite hormonal manipulation aimed at preventing it. Also called breakthrough ovulation.

Essure. A brand-name microinsert device used in a hysteroscopic sterilization procedure. The device is placed at the opening of each fallopian tube within the uterus, which causes scar tissue to block the tubes, keeping eggs and sperm from meeting.

Estrogen. A group of hormones that cause feminizing changes such as fatty deposits on the breasts and hips, higher voice, and lack of facial hair.

FDA. United States Food and Drug Administration, which regulates and approves medications.

Female condom. A barrier method of contraception in which a barrel-shaped bag with an open ring at the outside of the vagina permits penile entry, causing intercourse to take place inside the pouch so the ejaculate is blocked from reaching the cervical mucus.

Fertilization. The process in which the sperm penetrates the egg, resulting in a human zygote (one-cell embryo) at the moment when the chromosomes align and activate.

Fimbria. Fingerlike structures at the opening of the fallopian tube, near the ovary.

Folic acid. A common B vitamin known to reduce the risk of birth defects.

Follicle. A fluid-filled sac in the ovary that contains the egg to be released at ovulation.

Follicular phase. The portion of a woman's cycle prior to ovulation during which a follicle grows and high levels of estrogen cause the lining of the uterus to be lush and receptive to an embryo. The length of the follicular phase varies and can last between seven and twenty-one days.

FSH (follicle stimulating hormone). A pituitary hormone that stimulates sperm development in the male and follicular development in the female. Abnormally elevated levels of this hormone indicate failure of the reproductive glands in both men and woman.

Gamete. A reproductive cell—sperm in the man, ovum (or egg) in the woman.

Gestation. The carrying of a life within the uterus. Synonym: pregnancy.

Glans. Also called glans penis. Conical extremity, or head, of the penis.

Gonadotropin releasing hormone (GnRH). A hormone secreted by the hypothalamus approximately every ninety minutes, enabling the pituitary to secrete LH and FSH, which stimulate the gonads. See also FSH and LH.

Gonads. The glands (testicles, ovaries) that make reproductive cells (sperm, ova) and sex hormones (testosterone, estrogen).

Gossypol. A contraceptive agent made from cottonseed oil and readily available overseas, where it has been tested extensively. Men who have taken it have suffered from low potassium levels. Brand names include Nofertil.

HIV (human immunodeficiency virus). The virus that causes AIDS (acquired immunodeficiency syndrome).

HPV. See human papilloma virus.

Human papilloma virus (HPV). A sexually transmitted infection (STI) that, if untreated, causes genital warts and in some cases cervical cancer.

Hypothalamus. The brain's hormone regulation center.

Hysteroscopy. A procedure in which the doctor inserts a fiber-optic scope into the uterus to check for abnormalities. Minor surgical repairs can sometimes be done during this procedure.

Implanon. A brand-name female contraceptive implant that is long-acting (up to three years) and consists of a single rod placed under the skin of the arm. The implant must be inserted by a physician, and it can be removed at any time.

Implantation. The embedding of the embryo into tissue in the uterine wall so it can establish contact with the mother's blood supply. Implantation ideally occurs in the lining of the uterus; in an ectopic pregnancy, however, it occurs outside the uterus.

Infertility/primary infertility. The inability to conceive after one year of unprotected intercourse and/or the inability to carry a pregnancy to term.

Intrafallopian. Within the fallopian tubes.

IUD. See intrauterine device.

Intrauterine device (IUD). A device that is inserted and left in the uterus to prevent pregnancy. Several types of IUDs are available, including those containing chemicals (copper) and hormones (progesterone). IUDs may have an abortifacient effect.

Laparoscopy. A procedure in which a small telescope is inserted into an incision in the abdominal wall to view the internal organs. This allows diagnosis and treatment of a number of fertility problems, including endometriosis, abdominal adhesions, and polycystic ovaries. Also used by some clinics in egg retrieval for in vitro fertilization (IVF).

Levitra. A brand-name medication prescribed for erectile dysfunction.

Levonorgesterel A synthetic progesterone.

LH. See luteinizing hormone.

Lunelle. A brand-name female contraceptive made from a combination of estrogen and a progesterone derivative (a progestin, which is a synthetic hormone with activity similar to natural progesterone). Given in monthly injections.

Luteal phase. The postovulatory phase, or second half, of a woman's cycle. During this phase, the corpus luteum produces progesterone, making the uterine lining thicker so it can support the implantation and growth of an embryo.

Luteal phase defect (LPD). A deficiency in the amount of progesterone produced (or in the length of time it is produced) by the corpus luteum. An LPD can render the endometrium unable to sustain a pregnancy.

Luteinizing hormone (LH). A pituitary hormone that stimulates the gonads. In men, LH is necessary for sperm and testosterone production. In women, LH is necessary for progesterone production (FSH stimulates estrogen). When estrogen reaches its peak, the pituitary releases a surge of LH, which releases the egg from the follicle.

Masturbation. Manual stimulation of the sex organ, leading to orgasm. Male masturbation is used to collect semen for analysis.

Menstruation. The female's cyclical shedding of the uterine lining in response to stimulation from estrogen and progesterone.

Mini-laparotomy. Also called a mini-lap. A surgical approach to female sterilization done without use of a laparoscope.

Miscarriage. Spontaneous pregnancy loss (or spontaneous abortion) occurring within the first twenty weeks of pregnancy.

Morning-after pill. Also called emergency contraception. A series of oral contraceptives taken in a way that initially spike a woman's hormone levels. The patient then abruptly stops taking any pills, causing hormone levels to plummet. When used after ovulation, the morning-after pill works as an abortifacient. When used prior to ovulation, it is likely it will prevent ovulation.

Myometrium. The muscular portion of the uterine wall.

Natural family planning (NFP). In the context of contraception, natural family planning is a method of preventing pregnancy by careful monitoring of the bodily symptoms of ovulation in conjunction with planned periodic abstinence.

Neuroanatomy. The structural components of the nervous system, including the brain, spinal cord, and peripheral nerves, that are stimulated in response to heat and cold, pain, vibration, and pressure.

Neurochemistry. Chemical processes related to the nervous system; includes the group of neurotransmitters that affect neural functioning (response time, coordination, memory, mood, etc.).

NFP. See natural family planning.

Nifedipine. A medication often prescribed for high blood pressure and migraines that is being investigated for its ability to affect sperm cell membranes. Nifedipine appears to render sperm incapable of attaching themselves to the outer wall of the egg. Nifedipine also interferes with enzymes that enable sperm to penetrate the egg.

Nonoxynol-9. A spermicidal compound.

Norplant. A long-term (up to five years) female contraceptive method that involved the implanting of six thin, flexible plastic rods under the skin of the upper arm. Each rod contained a hormone (levonorgestrel) similar to the progesterone made by a woman's ovaries. Norplant is no longer available.

NuvaRing. A brand-name female contraceptive method that delivers hormones by means of a flexible vaginal ring.

OCP. Oral contraceptive pill.

Oocyte. An egg before maturation.

Orgasm. The psychological and physical thrill that accompanies sexual climax.

Os. See cervical os.

Ovaries. The female reproductive organs that produce eggs and female sex hormones.

Ovulation. Release of the mature egg (ovum) from an ovarian follicle.

Penis. The male sex organ.

POP. See progesterone-only pill.

Postpartum tubal. A type of female surgical sterilization procedure performed immediately following childbirth while the patient is still under the effects of the epidural or general anesthesia. A postpartum tubal can also be done within a day or two of delivery, using separate anesthesia. A small incision is made below the navel and extending into the abdominal cavity, and a loop of each fallopian tube is tied off and the intervening segment cut out.

Pituitary gland. The body's master hormonal gland that extends from the base of the brain and is stimulated by the hypothalamus. The pituitary controls all hormonal functions.

Progesterone-only pill (POP). An oral contraceptive pill that contains only the hormone progesterone.

Progestin. A synthetic progesterone.

Progestin DMPA (Progestin depot medroxyprogesterone acetate). Also known by the brand name Depo-provera. A long-acting hormonal contraceptive for women. It is currently being studied for its ability to stop sperm production in men. Normally given by injection.

Progesterone. The female sex hormone secreted by the corpus luteum during the second half of a woman's cycle (following ovulation). Progesterone thickens the lining of the uterus to prepare it to accept implantation of a fertilized egg and to sustain an ongoing pregnancy.

Prolactin. The hormone produced by the pituitary that stimulates production of milk in breastfeeding women. Excessive prolactin levels when a woman is not breastfeeding may result in infertility.

Quinacrine. A low-cost medication that has been used for decades to treat malaria. It is currently being investigated for its use in female nonsurgical permanent sterilization. Pellets of the medication are placed in the uterus near the openings to the fallopian tubes, where massive amounts of scar tissue form, blocking the egg and sperm from meeting.

Radiologist. A physician specializing in the use of radiant energy (such as X-rays and fluoroscopes) for diagnosis and testing.

Rh antibodies. The Rh system, discovered in Rhesus monkeys (hence the Rh), has to do with one class of antigens, which are proteins that evoke antibody response, on red blood cells. People who are

Rh positive carry this particular antigen; those who don't are Rh negative.

Rh immune globulin. The synthesized antibody given to Rh-negative women during pregnancy and to Rh-negative women who have delivered Rh-positive infants so the mothers do not develop their own antibodies, which might jeopardize the health of a future baby.

Reproductive cloning. Taking the genetic material from an "adult cell" (such as blood or skin) and placing it into a human egg from which the nucleus has been removed, then stimulating the cell with an electrical current or a chemical solution to "switch on" the proper cells for embryonic growth. After growing to the blastocyst stage, the embryo is transferred to a womb, where the embryo can implant and develop. Such cloning for the purpose of creating a child is illegal in many places, and it's considered immoral almost universally. See also therapeutic cloning.

RISUG (Reversible Inhibition of Sperm Under Guidance). A process, still being investigated, of injecting a compound into each vas deferens, which coats the inner wall of the ducts with a gel that has negative and positive electric charges. RISUG effectively renders sperm incapable of fertilizing an egg by rupturing the delicate membranes of sperm as they pass through the duct.

Rubella. German measles, responsible for birth defects in children whose mothers contract it while pregnant.

Semen. The fluid portion of the ejaculate, consisting of secretions from the seminal vesicles, prostate gland, and other glands in the male reproductive tract. It provides nourishment and protection for the sperm in a medium in which they can move freely. Semen may also refer to the entire ejaculate, including the sperm.

Shug. A brand-name contraceptive device that is injected by a physician into the vas deferens to block sperm from getting through. A silicone double plug with nylon tails, the Shug is still being studied.

Sonogram. An image of internal body parts that is produced by high-frequency sound waves. Sonograms are used to detect and count follicle growth (and disappearance) in many fertility treatments. They are also used to detect and monitor pregnancy. Also referred to as ultrasound.

Sonography. The use of ultrasound to create images of internal body parts.

Sperm count. The number of sperm in a man's ejaculate. Also called sperm concentration.

Spermicide. A sperm-killing product. Spermicides are available in foam, cream, jelly, film, suppository, or tablet form.

Spina bifida. A serious birth defect that involves incomplete development of the brain, the spinal cord, and/or the protective coverings of these organs.

Sponge. A barrier contraceptive made of polyurethane foam containing spermicide. The sponge is inserted into the vagina before sexual intercourse.

Sterilization reversal. A procedure done to restore fertility in a person who is sterile due to a surgical procedure done to prevent conception.

STI. Sexually transmitted infection.

Sterility. An irreversible condition that prevents conception.

Syngamy. The point at which chromosomes in the egg align with the chromosomes from the sperm and a one-cell being, a zygote, begins to divide and thrive.

Testicle. A male reproductive organ located in the scrotum.

Testosterone. The male hormone responsible for the formation of secondary sex characteristics (such as deep voice, sperm maturation, facial and body hair) and for supporting the sex drive. Testosterone is also necessary for sperm production.

Therapeutic cloning. Taking the genetic material from an "adult cell" (such as blood or skin) and placing it into a human egg from which the nucleus has been removed, then stimulating the cell with an electrical current or a chemical solution to "switch on" the proper cells for embryonic growth. Once the human embryo reaches the blastocyst stage, its embryonic cells are extracted for use in research, thereby killing the embryo. This differs from reproductive cloning in that the embryo is sacrificed for science rather than having the goal of creating a child. Both types of cloning violate several ethical principles.

Thyroid. An endocrine gland located in the neck that produces hormones necessary for fertility and other body functions.

Transvaginal sonogram. An image created by ultrasound and displayed on a TV screen. In transvaginal sonography, a delicately tapered ultrasound probe is inserted into the vagina to generate dramatic, detailed images of the pelvic anatomy.

Tubal. Relating to the fallopian tube. Also short for tubal ligation.

Tubal ligation. A surgical method of "permanent" sterilization in which both fallopian tubes are cut, cauterized with electricity, or clamped to prevent passage of the human egg to the uterus.

Tubal ostia. The mouth, or opening, of a fallopian tube at the uterus.

Tubal pregnancy. See ectopic pregnancy.

Ultrasound. In the context of infertility, ultrasound is a procedure in which a picture is displayed on a TV screen by bouncing sound waves off of the internal organs. Often used to monitor follicular development and to examine the fallopian tubes and uterus. Ultrasound is done both abdominally and transvaginally. See also sonography.

Unitive-procreative link. The belief that the act of intercourse (the "unitive") must always be joined with the potential for reproduction (the "procreative").

Urologist. A physician specializing in the genitourinary tract system, which includes primarily the urinary system (kidneys, bladder, and duct work).

Uterine ablation. Also called endometrial ablation. An outpatient surgical procedure to eliminate or reduce bleeding from the uterus by destroying the uterine lining by use of heated fluid, electrical cautery, or various types of laser.

Uterus. The womb. The hollow, muscular organ that houses and nourishes the fetus during pregnancy.

Vagina. The canal leading from the cervix to the outside of a woman's body; the birth passage.

Vas. Vas deferens.

Vas deferens. Tubes in the male reproductive system, measuring about two feet long, that serve as the ejaculatory ducts.

Vasectomy reversal. The attempt to restore the flow of sperm through the vas deferens after surgical sterilization.

Viagra. A brand-name medication prescribed for patients with erectile dysfunction.

Zygote. A fertilized egg that has not yet divided; the first cell of a new life.

Resources

Note: These resources do not necessarily reflect the views of the authors, of Zondervan, or of the Christian Medical Association.

Adoption

Adopt: Assistance Information Support:
www.adopting.org
Adoption:
www.adoption.com
Adoptive Families of America:
www.adoptivefamilies.com
National Adoption Information Clearinghouse:
www.calib.com/naic
National Council for Adoption:
www.ncfa-usa.org
North American Council on Adoptable Children:
www.nacac.org
Office of Children's Issues:
www.travel.state.gov/adopt.html
RainbowKids: International adoption information:
www.rainbowkids.com

Abstinence

Not Me, Not Now:
www.notmenotnow.com
Abstinence Educators' Network:
www.abednet.org
Teen Pregnancy:
www.teenpregnancy.org

General Information about Contraception and Contraceptives

All Health Links:
www.allhealthlinks.com
Christian Medical Association:
www.cmdahome.org
Family Health International:
www.fhi.org
FamilyLife:
www.familylife.com
Focus on the Family:
www.family.org
Alan Guttmacher Institute:
www.guttmacher.org
Young Women's Health:
www.youngwomenshealth.org
Women's Health:
www.womenshealth.about.com

Abstinence, Periodic Scheduled

Billings Ovulation Method:
www.billings-centre.ab.ca
Catholic Information Network:
www.cin.org/nfp.html
Couple to Couple League:
www.ccli.org
Natural Family Planning NZ:
www.natfamplan.co.nz
Downloadable Basal Body Temperature Charts:
www.harpnet.com/chart.html
Downloadable Natural Family Planning Chart:
www.harpnet.com/images/chart3.gif

Barrier Contraceptives

"Barrier Contraceptives: A Growing Array of Options." Health Square. http://www.healthsquare.com/fgwh/wh1ch19d.htm. This site has a variety of helpful diagrams.

Contraception Online
(site for clinicians, researchers, and educators):
www.contraceptiononline.org.
Women's Healthcare Center:
www.healthandage.com

Oral Contraceptives

Randy Alcorn. "Does the Pill Cause Abortions?"www.epm.org/
articles/bcpill2.html.
American Academy of Family Physicians:
www.aafp.org
Contraception.net web:
www.contraception.net

Emergency Contraception

American Life League:
www.all.org
The Morning-After Pill:
www.morningafterpill.org

Infertility

The authors' website:
www.aspire2.com
Conceiving Concepts:
www.conceivingconcepts.com
The International Council for Infertility Information Dissemination:
www.inciid.com
RESOLVE, Inc.:
www.resolve.org

Intrauterine Devices

Johns Hopkins Bloomberg School of Public Health:
www.jhuccp.org/topics/iuds.shtml
Reproductive Health Outlook:
www.rho.org/html/cont-iuds.htm

Sterilization

"Counseling Issues in Tubal Sterilization." American Academy of Family Physicians. www.aafp.org/afp/20030315/1287.pdf.
Family Health International:
www.fhi.org

Vatican Statement on Human Life

"Instruction on Respect for Human Life in Its Origin and on the Dignity of Procreation Replies to Certain Questions of the Day." www.vatican.va/roman_curia/congregations/cfaith/docments/rc_con_cfaith_doc_19870222_respect-for-human-life_en.html.

Analysis of the Vatican Statement

Luke Timothy Johnson. "A Disembodied 'Theology of the Body': John Paul II on Love, Sex and Pleasure." *Commonwealth*, January 2001. Published by Commonwealth Foundation, 475 Riverside Drive, Room 405, New York, NY 10115, (212) 662-4200.

Related Titles

William Cutrer, M.D. *Under the Fig Leaves.* Bristol, TN: Paul Tournier Institute of the Christian Medical Association, 2002.

William Cutrer, M.D., and Sandra Glahn. *Sexual Intimacy in Marriage.* Grand Rapids: Kregel, 2001.

Sandra Glahn, Th.M., and William Cutrer, M.D. *The Infertility Companion.* Grand Rapids: Zondervan, 2004.

Sandra Glahn and William Cutrer, M.D. *When Empty Arms Become a Heavy Burden.* Nashville: Broadman and Holman, 1997.

INDEX

Page numbers in italics indicate glossary entries.

breast cancer, 96, 204n. 5, 205n. 9
breastfeeding and contraception, 31–32, 56–57

calendar method, 56
cancer
    risk of, 93, 96
    and vasectomy, 150
cervical cap, 81–83, *212*
cervical mucus, *212*
    changes in, 67, 89
    checking the, 58–60, 63, 66
cervical os, 63, *212*
cervix, 44, 63, *212*
chemicals, 71, 77
children
    within the context of family, 49
    devaluation of, 177
    and Jesus, 175
    number of, 21
    in Old Testament cultures, 172–74
Christian Medical and Dental Associations (CMDA), 111
    statements, 193–99
chromosome, *212*
cilia, *212*
clitoris, 39, 44, *212*
cloning, 202n. 9, *213*
    reproductive, *221*
    therapeutic, *222*
clotting, risk of, 93
COCs (combination oral contra-ceptives), 91–92, 95–97, 113, *213*. *See also* birth control pills; OCPs; pill, the; POPs
coitus interruptus, 30, 55, *213*
combination oral contraceptives. *See* COCs

communication
    about conception, 189–90
    improving, 41
conception, considering, 189, *213*
condoms, *213*
    deterioration of, 31
    for him, 72–75
    how to use, 30
    for her, 75–77
    in the seventeenth century, 26
contraception, *213*
    abortion as, 177–78
    attitudes toward, 154
    and breastfeeding, 31–32, 56–57
    chemical approaches to, 77
    communication about, 189
    the future of, 153
    repugnant methods of, 26
    spiritual implications of, 165
    as unethical, 36
contraceptive foam, 77
contraceptive patch, *213*
cornua, *213*
corpus luteum, *213*
cryopreservation, 197–99
cysts, 96, 99

de Becker, Gavin, 40
deoxyribonucleic acid (DNA), 48, 202n. 9, *214*
Depo-Provera, 120–21, 155
depot medroxyprogesterone acetate (DMPA), 155
diaphragm, 27, 80–81, *214*
DNA (deoxyribonucleic acid), 48, 202n. 9, *214*
dopamine, 202n. 1
douching, 31

ectopic pregnancy, 135, *214*
eggs, 44–45, 47–49
    maturation of, 87, 87–88
    number of, 96
ejaculation, 44, 47, 73, *214*
embryos, 89, 91, 119, *214*
    at risk, 101–5
emergency contraception, 118–20, *214*. *See also* morning-after pill
endometrial ablation, *214*
endometriosis, 99, 108, *214*
endometrium, 108, 137, *215. See also* uterine lining
endorphins, 43–44, *215*
epididymis, 46, *215*
erection, 44, *215*
erythromycin, 159–60, *215*
escape ovulation, 101, *215*
Essure, 135–37, *215*
estrogen, 41, 45, 46, 86–88, *215*

faith, 54, 68
fallopian tubes, 47, 86, 130, 133
family
    adding to your, 179
    blueprint for, 165–70
    decisions about, 189
    importance of, 177
    as an independent unit, 174
    in the New Testament, 175
    in Old Testament time, 172
FamilyLife Manifesto, 201n. 1
family planning, 201n. 1
family size, 66
FDA (Federal Drug Administration), *215*
female condom, 77, *215*
female reproductive cycle, 86
female sterilization, 130–31
fertility, 44, 56, 88

fertilization, 46–48, 193, 197, *215*
fimbria, *215*
foams, 78
folic acid, *216*
follicle, *216*
follicle cysts, 88, 104
follicle stimulating hormone (FSH), 87–90, *216*
follicular phase, *216*
FSH (follicle stimulating hormone), 87–90, *216*

gamete, *216*
Genesis, 37
genetic counseling, 181
gestation, *216*
glans, *216*
GnRH (gonadotropin releasing hormone), *216*
God
    image of, 166, 169
    intimacy with, 175–76
gonadotropin releasing hormone (GnRH), *216*
gonads, *216*
gossypol, 158, *216*

heart attack, 93
hepatitis, 181
herbs, 27
herpes, 77. *See also* STIs
HIV (human immunodeficiency virus), 181, *216*
hormonal contraceptives, 90
hormones
    body secretes, 44–46
    combination of, 91–92
    injected, 115
    messenger, 47
    two key, 87
    women and, 113

spermicides, 49, 73, 75, 77, 79, 81, 222
sperm production, methods that inhibit, 74
spina bifida, 222
sponge, the, 78–80, 222
sterility, 222
sterilization
    for her, 140
    permanent, 129, 132
    pros and cons of, 141
    reasons for, 131–32
    risk factors of, 138
sterilization reversals, 139, 222
STIs (sexually transmitted infections), 74, 77, 181, 222
stroke, risk of, 96
surgical contraception, pros and cons of, 138
sympto-thermal method, 61
syngamy, 48–49, 202n. 9, 222

temperature charting method, 61
testicles, 46, 222
testosterone, 41, 45–46, 222
    plummeting levels of, 155
therapeutic cloning, 222
thyroid, 223
transvaginal sonogram, 223
triphasic pills, 92
tubal ligation, 130–34, 223
    postpartum, 133, 219
    reversing, 133, 141
tubal ostia, 223
tubal pregnancy, 223
tuberculosis, 181
tubes tied. See tubal ligation

ultrasound, 105–6, 223
unitive-procreative link, 35–36, 223
urologist, 223
uterine ablation, 137, 223
uterine lining, 88, 205n. 8. See also endometrium
    altering the, 120
    destroying the, 137
    and the pill, 102
    thinning of the, 103, 107–8
uterus, 44, 48, 86, 224
    removing the, 131

vagina, 44, 47, 86, 224
vaginal infections, 66
vaginal ring, 117–18
Vasclip, 145
vas deferens, 224
vasectomy, 49, 143–52. See also vasectomy reversal
    pros and cons of, 151
    and prostate disease, 147
vasectomy reversal, 133, 141, 149, 224
Vatican statement, 35
Viagra, 224
vulva, 44

withdrawal method, 54–56. See also coitus interruptus

X-rays, 181

yeast infections, 66

Zoloft, 202n. 2
zygote, 224

Christian
Medical
Association
Resources

Medically reliable ... biblically sound. That's the rock-solid promise of this series offered by Zondervan in partnership with the Christian Medical Association. Each book in this series is not only written by fully credentialed, experienced doctors but is also fully reviewed by an objective board of qualified doctors to ensure its reliability. Because when your health is at stake, you can't settle for anything less than the whole and accurate truth.

Integrating your faith and health can improve your physical well-being and even extend your life, as you gain insights into the interconnection of health and faith—a relationship largely overlooked by secular science. Benefit from the cutting-edge knowledge of respected medical experts as they help you make health care decisions consistent with your beliefs. Their sound biblical analysis of emerging treatments and technologies equips you to protect yourself from seemingly harmless—yet spiritually, ethically, or medically unsound—options and then to make the healthiest choices possible.

Through this series, you can draw from both the knowledge of science and the wisdom of God's Word in addressing your medical ethics decisions and in meeting your health care needs.

Founded in 1931, the Christian Medical Association helps thousands of doctors minister to their patients by imitating the Great Physician, Jesus Christ. Christian Medical Association members provide a Christian voice on medical ethics to policy makers and the media, minister to needy patients on medical missions around the world, evangelize and disciple students on more than 90 percent of the nation's medical school campuses, and provide educational and inspirational resources to the church.

To learn more about Christian Medical Association ministries and resources on health care and ethical issues, browse the website (www.christian medicalassociation.org) or call toll-free at 1-888-231-2637.

"Dear friend, I pray that you may enjoy good health and that all may go well with you, even as your soul is getting along well" (3 John 2).

We want to hear from you. Please send your comments about this
book to us in care of zreview@zondervan.com. Thank you.

GRAND RAPIDS, MICHIGAN 49530 USA

WWW.ZONDERVAN.COM